# DOMINION!

DESTINY IMAGE BOOKS BY C. PETER WAGNER

*Breaking Spiritual Strongholds in Your City*

*Let's Laugh*

*Warfare Prayer*

*Praying with Power*

*Spiritual Warfare Strategy*

*Territorial Spirits*

*Supernatural Forces in Spiritual Warfare*

*6 Secrets to Living a Fruitful Life*

*Praying for the America of Tomorrow*

*Reformer's Pledge* (contributor)

*Prayer Changes Things* (contributor)

# DOMINION!

## YOUR ROLE IN BRINGING
## HEAVEN TO EARTH

## C. PETER WAGNER

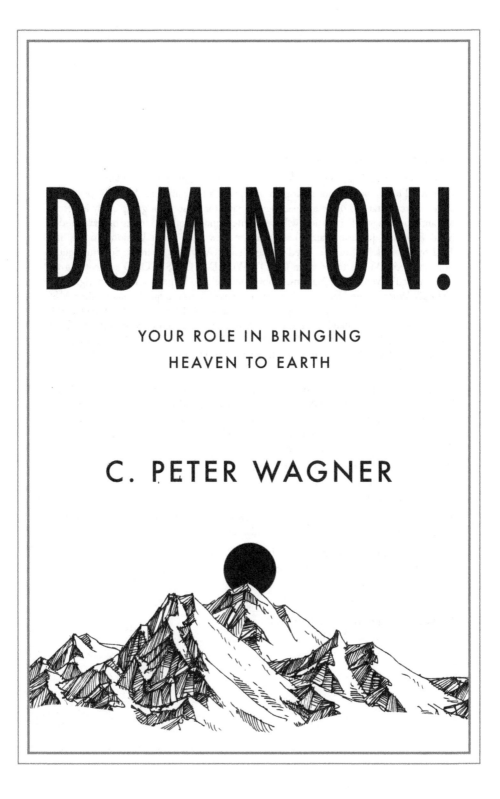

DESTINY IMAGE® PUBLISHERS, INC.
P.O. Box 310, Shippensburg, PA 17257-0310
*"Promoting Inspired Lives."*

This book and all other Destiny Image and Destiny Image Fiction books are available at Christian bookstores and distributors worldwide.

For more information on foreign distributors, call 717-532-3040.
Reach us on the Internet: www.destinyimage.com.

ISBN 13 TP: 978-0-7684-6164-0
ISBN 13 eBook: 978-0-7684-6165-7

For Worldwide Distribution, Printed in the U.S.A.
1 2 3 4 5 6 7 8 / 26 25 24 23 22

# CONTENTS

# CONTENTS

# A NOTE FROM THE PUBLISHER

Dominion! Such a title surely provokes an array of responses from Christian and unbeliever alike, especially when someone is slightly familiar with the concept of "dominion theology." This timeless work from the late Dr. C. Peter Wagner was published originally under the title, *Dominion!* and then republished as *As It Is in Heaven.* I sensed an assignment to return to the original title, as dominion is the missing link between revival and reformation.

When people are personally or corporately revived by the Holy Spirit, it's not for a "zing and a thrill." It's not so they can become dependent on spiritual "IV fluid" (a.k.a. conferences, gatherings, events). We believe in these things for the sake of sending those touched by the power of God into whatever spheres of influence they have been called and assigned to.

Most recently, we witnessed what happened when revival did not produce societal reformation. In the 1960s and '70s, you had the Charismatic Renewal and the Jesus People movements, both of which significantly impacted the landscape of the church. And yet, there was an underlying narrative, throughout that era, causing believers to focus more on the imminent return of Jesus than actually being salt and light in the world they had been assigned to. Thus, Christians disengaged from society, and today we have inherited the fruit of that disengagement. But things are truly shifting!

*Dominion* is not about Christians taking over the planet; it's about people filled with the Holy Spirit serving the world they have been assigned to. It's about the people of God improving and bettering the quality of life for the whole of society. It's about carrying the Presence of God and the solutions of His Kingdom to every realm that has been influenced by darkness.

It's a joy to republish this timely work for this most urgent hour.

LARRY SPARKS
Publisher, Destiny Image
November 2021

# PREFACE

Some might suggest that the book you have in your hands should carry a warning label as if it were a shipment of spiritually radioactive materials. In a moment or two you will see what I mean.

If you are like me, you frequently skip the "Preface" or the "Introduction" to the book you pick up in order to get right into the meat of what the author is saying. My advice? Don't do it with this book! Please let me explain why.

To my knowledge—limited knowledge to be sure—this has never happened to another book. You see, I had been personal friends with the editor of one of the most respected evangelical publishers for years, but they had never published any of my books. Finally, a few years ago, they offered me a very generous financial package for my next book, which I decided to allow them to publish. We began the one-year-plus process of writing, editing, rewriting, artwork, copyrighting, cover design, marketing, setting a release date, and spreading the word to the bookstores through catalogs and via Internet. The release date was approaching and the hardback copies of the book were produced, packed, and ready to be shipped to bookstores and outlets across the country. My friend and I were very excited!

But, no! Someone higher up in the company that owned my publisher suddenly decided to trash the book! They cancelled the orders from the bookstores and prohibited sales through any of their distribution networks. They must have felt quite strongly that this was an unacceptable book because they were willing to take a considerable financial hit to pull it from circulation. Not only did they lose my author's advance, but their costs in terms of labor and materials to get a title like that on the market would be hard to absorb into the average budget. They remaindered the copies they had on hand, which means that they sold what they could in quantities to private distributors at fire-sale prices.

Why? What was going on? This was as much of a shock to my friend, who was the editor, as it was to me! I tried my best to get the company to open up and tell me what had really transpired behind the scenes to precipitate such a radical decision, but to no avail. I received nothing but polite, evasive responses. To this day I have not even heard the hint of a leak as to why my book might have been rejected.

## An Inquisitive Mind

I have a fairly inquisitive mind. This means that I am not usually satisfied with polite, evasive answers. My recourse, therefore, is to attempt to come up with the best educated guess possible, and I have been working on that for quite some time. I want to emphasize the word guess. The risk I am taking is that I might be wrong, and, unless some leak does occur, we may never know. So, what is the guess?

Let's start with the title of the book. It was a one-word title, *Dominion!*, with the exclamation point as part of the title. The subtitle was *How Kingdom Action Can Change the World*. This immediately would bring up the issue of reforming society. My underlying premise is that it is the will of God that His people here on earth take dominion of the society in which they live, promoting the values and the blessings and the prosperity of the kingdom of God for everyone. You will read about this in considerable detail as you go through the book.

I have been working on what I like to call "the dominion mandate" since the mid-1990s. This required a radical paradigm shift for me because previously I did not consider becoming involved with society as a God-given assignment for the church. But once I shifted, I began my usual modus operandi of researching and teaching the related issues and finally organizing my thoughts in a book. As I was writing the book, I was aware that not all of my friends, even those who joined me in the charismatically inclined evangelical stream, would agree with all the conclusions I was reaching. I expected the book to stimulate some creative tensions and fruitful dialogs, which would help us all hear better what God was saying to the churches today.

## Underestimating Opposition

I now see that I severely underestimated the degree of opposition that had already developed in certain circles against the dominion mandate. In fact, I am embarrassed to admit that a network of Christian apologists had been opposing what they called "dominionism" for some time, and when I wrote my book I had not yet even heard the term nor read what they were writing. What were they saying? Let me just cherry-pick from the Internet some of their descriptive phrases relating to dominionism: a "dangerous political movement," "religious extremism," "a betrayal of the political and social mores of our society," "hate mongering," "bizarre ideas of a handful of Christian Right players," "aberration of true Christian theology," "heresy," "Christian imperialism," just for starters.

The more I have read and analyzed this material, the more convinced I have become that fear is one of the principal driving elements underlying the sincere opposition by some to dominionism. While there are many other specific objects of fear pinpointed in the literature, most all of them can be summarized in the fear that dominionism will lead to a theocracy. Oddly enough, I am as apprehensive of a theocracy as they are, and I will explain this shortly.

But meanwhile, remember the publisher who trashed this book? Suppose he or she had been influenced by the anti-dominionism movement. Suppose the fear of advocating a theocracy was a determining factor. If so, the release of a book whose title was *Dominion!* could pose, in that person's mind, a legitimate threat to our entire American society, to say nothing of the reputation of the publisher. Operating from such a mindset, withholding the book from the market, regardless of the cost, could be considered a reasonable decision to make.

I repeat that the above is simply a guess. But it is a scenario that could well fit the circumstances involved.

# The Resurrection of a Book

Now, let's get back to the book itself. In the interim, quite a few individuals ended up with copies of the controversial book because a number of independent booksellers were able to buy some of the remainders and resell them on the Internet. A flurry of public interest surfaced in mid-2011 when Governor Rick Perry announced as a candidate for the Republican nomination for President. Some of his opponents found ways of associating him with dominionism, and the Internet lit up with animated discussions of the matter for around three months. Time magazine ran a cover story on Governor Perry, accompanied by an article, "In God We Trust: Few in number, dominionists believe the Bible should govern society." The article says, "What is new in the 2012 race is the emergence of the New Apostolic Reformation (NAR), which was named by C. Peter Wagner, a Colorado Springs-based minister who writes books with titles like Dominion! How Kingdom Action Can Change the World and believes the world is in the grip of evil...The NAR's mission: to achieve dominion over the darkness through Christian activism in politics and beyond."[1] In essence, the article states our purpose quite accurately.

Please allow me to say it in my own words:

# A Foundation for Our Mandate

I have written Dominion! to provide a biblical, theological, and strategic foundation in order to help undergird the urgent mandate of God for the church to actively engage in transforming society. As I have said, this is a relatively new paradigm for most of us, both in the nuclear church and in the extended church of the workplace. In order to get the big picture, I will try to pull together many important conceptual threads such as the biblical government of the church (i.e., apostles and prophets), dominion or kingdom theology, an open view of God, the church in the workplace, the great transfer of wealth, and other related themes.

My basic premise is that God's kingdom should come and that His will should be done here on earth as it is in heaven. This is clearly a Christian principle because these are the very words that Jesus taught His disciples to pray every day in the Lord's Prayer. What would this look like? Every segment of the society in which we live would be permeated with the peace and justice and prosperity and health and righteousness and joy and harmony and love and freedom that characterize God's original design for human life. All earthly societies, including our own U.S., would be happier and more fulfilled with these qualities of life fully realized than without them. With this, you can see why my book's title is *Dominion!* While all committed Christians will embrace these values, Christians are not the only ones who do so. Many non-Christians also agree that the societies in which we live should move in the direction I have just described, and they also want to participate personally in such a transformation.

Obviously, right now we all find ourselves on earth—not yet in heaven. Consequently, we must follow certain earthly rules if we are going to change our society for the good. A starting point is to recognize what many of us have been calling the "Seven Mountains," which are the supreme molders of culture: Religion, Family, Education, Media, Government, Arts & Entertainment, and Business. For a given society to change, each one of the Seven Mountains needs to be influenced or "dominated" by persons of goodwill, whether Christians or non-Christians. This is a positive way of looking at dominionism.

My hope is that those who agree with God's ideal for human life will be those who find themselves, at the end of the day, in positions of influence over society, whether it be within cities or states or nations or other territories and people groups. The biblical ideology underlying this vision is called "dominion theology," which I explain in some detail in Chapter 3.

## Not a Theocracy!

As I mentioned earlier, the overriding fear on the part of those who oppose dominionism is that it might end up advocating a theocracy. For example, the Religious Freedom Coalition produced a paper with the apprehensive title, "Could There Be a Theocracy in America's Future?"[2] Though well researched, the paper draws the questionable conclusion that dominion theology threatens to open the door I have just described, leading to a much-dreaded theocracy in our country.

The fear is so pervasive that a substantial book by Kevin Phillips carries the title *American Theocracy*. This is an attempt to heighten the theophobia characterizing many Americans today. One of Phillips' major culprits in supposedly moving America toward a theocracy was George W. Bush, who was bold enough to affirm his faith in God publicly as well as his desire to hear from God and do His will for the nation from time to time. Phillips fears a "strongly leader-driven theocracy" and refers to "George W. Bush, Theocrat-in-Chief."[3]

I must admit that certain individuals in the circles with which I identify have, perhaps in moments of over enthusiasm, made statements that could be interpreted as advocating theocracy. This is regrettable, but understandable. In calmer discussions of the issues involved, none of them, to my knowledge, would suggest that any human government should be a theocracy.

## What Is Theocracy?

Theocracy means a government headed up by God. Those of us who believe the Bible agree that the whole earth will someday be ruled by God. Since God is the Creator of the universe, He has the ultimate right to rule. Jesus Christ, the Second Person of the Trinity, is predicted by the Bible to return to earth once again, not as a sacrifice on the cross, but this time as a warrior on a white horse. He will take charge of human society once and for all, and when that happens, we will experience a new earth different from anything we have known since Adam and Eve.

However, all of this is in the future. No one knows when this will happen. It may be in our generation, it may be many generations from now. Meanwhile, we humans who represent God have the responsibility of doing the best we can, with all of our shortcomings and imperfections, to establish human societies that, as far as possible, reflect the blessings of God on all of humanity. In my opinion, the best way to accomplish this is through a democracy, not a theocracy.

Human history is replete with experiments in theocratic government, both Christian and non-Christian. Today the most prominent examples would be Muslim nations under *sharia* law, which is Islamic law based on the Qur'an. The god—or *theos*—supposedly governing those societies is Allah, who by no stretch of the imagination should be confused with Jehovah God, the Father of Jesus Christ. I need not catalog the long list of officially sanctioned violations of human rights inherent (not just accidental) in *sharia* law. Worth mentioning, however, just as an example are laws against the crime of "apostasy," which include (among other things) leaving Islam for another faith such as Christianity, and which prescribe capital punishment by stoning or beheading. Religious freedom is not considered a human right under Islamic theocracies.

When America gained independence from England, it separated itself from a state church that was essentially a form of theocracy. In theory, God was the ruler over England, and the king or queen was seen as God's appointed head. In turn, the monarch appointed the Archbishop of Canterbury, who was over the Church of England or the Anglican Church. Our American Constitution broke from this tradition and prohibited the U.S. government from establishing a state church like the Anglican Church—effectively ruling out a theocracy. Democracy took the place of theocracy/monarchy, and democracy has worked very well, at least for America, for over two hundred years.

That is why I would reject not only a theocracy, but even more so an imagined "ecclesiocrcacy" in which the church would rule. The church is instructed not to go in this direction by Romans 13:1-4. Referring to the government of the Roman Empire, Paul wrote: *Let every soul be subject to the governing authorities. For there is no authority except from God, and the authorities that exist are appointed by God"* (Rom. 13:1). Returning for a moment to the "Seven Mountain Template," the church, as an organized body, should recognize that its activities and influence operate in the Religion Mountain, not in any of the other six. Civil government should be seen as a function of the Government Mountain, and the two should not be confused.

None of this detracts from the central thesis of this book that God's plan is for His kingdom to come to earth as it is in heaven right in the here and now. This means that kingdom-minded and kingdom-motivated individuals in all seven of the mountains must strive toward influencing and taking dominion of whatever sphere of society God has assigned them. When this is applied to the Government Mountain, it means that God's people with high biblical standards should seek to occupy the highest possible government offices within whatever form of government they find themselves. This is biblical dominionism, but not theocracy.

## Democracy Works!

Democracy has proven to be the best choice for civil government because of its built-in checks and balances that help counteract the inherent sinful nature of individuals passed down to us since Adam's fall. Let's look more closely at how taking dominion of society and infusing the values of the kingdom of God can operate within a democratic government.

Democracy, by definition, is a government of the people, by the people, and for the people. In a democracy, while there is no established religion, religious people can be elected to office as freely as can non-religious people, and they can also rise to the highest and most influential positions in any of the Seven Mountains. If Christians win elections, gain influence, and occupy pubic offices, it should be expected that they will propagate and implement their values. This is not theocracy; it is a normal outworking of democracy. I agree with Rick Joyner who says, "You can have the best form of government and still have bad government if you have bad people in it. God is seeking to write His laws on the heart of people. The form of government is the scaffolding, but the character of the people is the real government."[4]

Christians understand that kingdom values should penetrate all areas of their personal lives, their families, their businesses, their political choices, and the rest. While we in America constitutionally avoid a state church, we must never imagine it possible to separate a person's religion or faith from the way he or she thinks and decides and votes and governs on all issues of life. Anyone who would vote contrary to his or her spiritual values would be a hypocrite, thereby disqualified from public office on the grounds of defective character.

Freedom and personal liberty are part and parcel of a government undergirded by godly kingdom principles. Consequently, people of other religious faiths or those who have no faith at all are welcomed and respected. Each one has a vote. True democracy honors religious pluralism. If those of a certain faith are a majority, they are expected to elect leaders who share their values. If they are a minority, however, they should not expect to rule.

If Christian principles happen to be directing the government, freedom of non-Christians is essential. Why? Because people are Christians only because they have made that personal choice. True believers are not born into their faith—they are believers as a result of their personal decision to open their lives to Jesus Christ. That is what "born again" means. No true Christian was ever taken hostage and forced to convert as a price for his or her release. Nor do people remain Christian out of fear that if they apostatize they will be subject to capital punishment as those under *sharia* law. Christians have no reason to put non-Christians in jail or deny them civil rights simply because they have decided not to be born again but instead to follow other religions. Religious freedom is highly valued in God's kingdom here on earth.

## The Majority Rules

To clarify a bit further, if Christians happen to constitute the majority in a democratic society, they will respect the rights of minorities. They will not, however—in a true democracy—be expected to support anti-Christian minority desires to mold society according to non-Christian values. Nor will they feel intimidated by those who proclaim that religion should never be mixed with politics. They will agree with Barak Obama, who said, "Secularists are wrong when they ask believers to leave their religion at the door before entering the public square."[5]

For example, if a Christian majority wants to allow praying to God in the name of Jesus in certain public gatherings, the minority should follow the basic rules of democracy and not attempt to prohibit such a practice. If a majority feels that heterosexual marriage is the best choice for a happy and prosperous society, those in the minority who might disagree should conform—not because they live in a theocracy, but because they live in a democracy. The most basic principle of democracy is that the majority of the people, not the minority, rules and sets the ultimate norms for society.

In light of this, taking dominion or transforming society does not imply a theocracy. Dominionism comes about through playing by the rules of the democratic game, and, fairly and squarely through the votes of the people, gaining the necessary influence in the Seven Mountains to ultimately benefit the whole nation and open all of society for the blessings, prosperity, and happiness God desires for all people. Kingdom-minded people, not the organized church, will govern the transformed societies of the future. Once again, this is not a plea for a theocracy.

## The Components of Social Transformation

Back in 2005, I believe it was God Himself who revealed to me a graphic depicting the essential components for transforming society. In the chapters that follow, I will explain them and show how they interrelate.

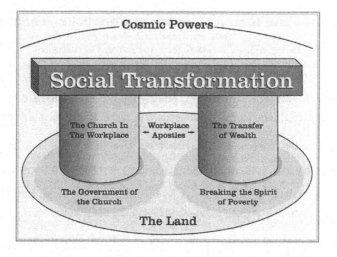

Social transformation, as depicted on the graphic, is supported by two major pillars. The first is "The Church in the Workplace." This idea began to take shape across the body of Christ in the late 1990s, and it became common currency in the 2000s. In 2006 I published a textbook on the subject, *The Church in the Workplace* (Regal Books, 2006), and I also summarize this concept further in Chapter 7 of this book. The foundation of the first pillar is "The Biblical Government of the Church." My textbook on that subject is *Apostles Today* (Regal Books, 2007), which I touch on in Chapter 1.

The second pillar is "The Great Transfer of Wealth," which God has been promising through His prophets for several years. In Chapter 9, I point out that throughout human history, three things above all have transformed society: violence, knowledge, and wealth—and the greatest of these is wealth. Without vast amounts of wealth in the hands of kingdom-minded people who line up with the principles of the kingdom of God, I am convinced we will not see the social transformation that we desire. The foundation of this pillar is "Breaking the Spirit of Poverty." Unfortunately, large segments of the church imagine that there is a direct correlation between piety and poverty. This is a crippling delusion. We must cast out the spirit of poverty and replace it with the godly spirit of prosperity if we expect to act as effective agents of social transformation.

"Workplace Apostles" are the dynamic catalysts who will activate the whole process. In Chapter 7 I explain this important piece of the puzzle and why we cannot expect to see sustained social transformation without activating our workplace apostles.

"The Land" underlying the whole structure and "The Cosmic Powers" hovering over it highlight the necessity of taking spiritual warfare seriously. As the leader of the forces of darkness, Satan hates the idea of righteous social transformation. He has come to steal, to kill, and to destroy (see John 10:10). He does not want people being happy and prosperous. Poverty and misery are the devil's strong suits. I spell out the principles and practices of dealing with this in Chapter 6, entitled "A New Reality: This Means War!"

The task before us is enormous—but it is exciting! There has never been a better time in history to love God and to act as one of His agents in helping mold the earth in a way that will fulfill His true destiny for the human race. My prayer is that this book will impart to every reader a passion for action and the faith to believe that what we decide to do will make a difference in the lives of multitudes of people.

Chapter 1

# A NEW WINE: THE
# SECOND APOSTOLIC AGE

We who are Christian believers now live in the most extraordinarily exciting time in all of human history!

I know that some will be saying that this is a rather preposterous statement. But let's think about it for a few moments.

## Communications Superhighway

It is true that history has been peppered with many extraordinary times. However, only this current generation has possessed the communications superhighway. Nobody even knows when, how, and where the wheel was first invented. Millions of people in China and Africa and India did not know or did not even care that Columbus discovered America. It was a long, slow process for the changes to come about initiated by Isaac Newton discovering the law of gravity or the Wright brothers flying an airplane at Kitty Hawk or Henry Ford installing the first assembly line to affect the way large numbers of people live.

Christian history has also seen some extraordinary times beginning with Jesus' incarnation, crucifixion, and resurrection, then moving through the Acts of the Apostles and the Christianization of the Roman Empire and the Protestant Reformation and the Modern Missionary Movement and the Azusa Street Revival, just to name a few high points. Each one of these caused great excitement, but, at least initially, among only a relatively small segment of the Christian population of the day.

Now that the whole world is in touch with each other through cyberspace, our situation is vastly different. When the Holy Spirit speaks to the churches, apostles on all continents who have an ear to hear will be in agreement with what God is saying about the next season of the church. This in itself would make it an exciting time to be alive, but just as significant is the fact that the church of Jesus Christ is now in the beginning phases of the most radical change in the way of doing church since the Protestant Reformation of the 16th century.

What, exactly, is this change?

## The Second Apostolic Age

In a word, we are now in the Second Apostolic Age. We have been here, to the best of my calculation, since around 2001. For the first time this side of the initial couple of centuries of the church, a critical mass of the body of Christ once again recognizes the contemporary gifts and offices of apostle and prophet. Growing numbers of people have come to take literally Ephesians 2:20, which says that the foundation of the church is apostles and prophets with Jesus the chief cornerstone.

As is the case with every significant paradigm shift such as this one, not everyone changes at once. Sociologists employ diffusion of innovation theory to measure such things. This turns out to be a bell-shaped curve that helps predict rates of change, moving across time from the innovators to early adopters, middle adopters, late adopters, and finally laggards who never change. The New Apostolic Reformation, a blanket term for churches in the Second Apostolic Age, is currently in the early adopter phase at least in America. That is why you will still find many churches and denominations that have not yet even heard of the New Apostolic Reformation as well as many others that may know something about it but who have decided for various reasons that they do not want to participate, at least not yet.

## A Massive Movement

Still, it is important to know up front that this is a massive movement, recognized widely by sociologists of religion and by church historians and by other scholars as well. For example, one of our most respected researchers, David Barrett, author of the massive World Christian Encyclopedia, has divided world Christianity into five[1] "megablocks," the largest of which is Roman Catholicism with over one billion members. However, of the four non-Catholic megablocks, the New Apostolic Reformation (which he calls Neo-Apostolic or Independent or Postdenominational) is the largest with over 432 million adherents, compared to smaller numbers for the Protestant/Evangelical, Orthodox, and Anglican mega-blocks.[2] These Neo-Apostolics comprised only 3 percent of non-Catholic Christianity in 1900, but they are projected to include almost 50 percent by 2025.

Not only is the New Apostolic Reformation the largest of the four non-Catholic megablocks, but, significantly enough, it is the only one of all five that is growing faster than Islam. It is important to recognize that we are not talking about something on the fringes, but we are talking about a dynamic movement at the very heart of 21st century Christianity.

The roots of the New Apostolic Reformation can be traced back as far as 1900 when the African Independent Church Movement was first launched. The Chinese House Church Movement beginning around 1975 and the Latin American Grassroots Church Movement emerging around 1980 were parts of the same spiritual phenomenon on different continents. In the U.S., the independent charismatic churches, dating back to around 1970, were the most immediate precursors of what is now called the New Apostolic Reformation.

## Theological Bedrock

When I said that we are now living in the most radical change in the way of doing church since the Protestant Reformation, I want to stress the phrase "doing church." The core theology of the Reformation is not what is currently being changed; rather, it continues to provide the theological bedrock upon which the New Apostolic Reformation is built. Martin Luther set in place the final authority of Scripture for faith and practice, when previously the institutional church itself had been considered the final authority. He established the biblical principle of justification by faith rather than salvation by good works. He taught the priesthood of all believers. The older idea was that Christians needed an ordained priest in order to help them get to God. Luther said no. Every believer can and should approach God and communicate with Him without requiring the mediation of a professional priest.

That was back in the 16th century. A couple hundred years later, in the 18th century, John Wesley clarified biblical principles of personal holiness, which the reformers had not emphasized in the same way. The 19th century then saw the blossoming of the Modern Missionary Movement, starting with William Carey going to India driven by the controversial principle of "using means," as he stated it, to reach the heathen.[3] The renowned Azusa Street Revival of 1906 finally began to bring the person and work of the Third Person of the Trinity, the Holy Spirit, into His proper place. In fact, here in the United States, the genealogy of the New Apostolic Reformation is traced through the independent charismatic churches, then back through classical Pentecostalism, and finally to the Azusa Street Revival.

## Intercessors, Prophets, and Apostles

A significant acceleration of the historical process leading to the Second Apostolic Age began in the decade of the 1970s. This is when the great prayer movement began. Virtually every notable prayer movement on today's scene started this side of 1970. For the first time, the body of Christ began recognizing the gift and office of intercessor. Today one can go into churches virtually across the denominational spectrum and be introduced to So-and-So with the words, "She is one of our intercessors." In the 1970s and before, this would have been extremely rare, although "prayer warriors" were sometimes acknowledged; but the newer trend of recognizing and activating intercessors in our churches and ministries continues to grow.

The gift and office of prophet began to be affirmed by the body of Christ in the decade of the 1980s. By saying this, I do not mean to imply that there were no prophets before 1980. I believe that the church has always had prophets. However, previous to the 1980s most prophets of God were restricted in their ministry by the widespread notion among many believers that the office of prophet had ceased after the first century or so. Now, however, a growing critical mass of the church recognizes and affirms the office of prophet.

The decade of the 1990s saw the beginning of the recognition of the gift and office of apostle in today's church. True, many Christian leaders do not as yet believe that we now have legitimate apostles on the level of Peter or Paul or John, but a critical mass of the church agrees that they are here. For example, at this writing the International Coalition of Apostles (ICA), over which I presided for ten years, includes over five hundred members who mutually recognize and affirm each other as legitimate apostles.

## The Sequence

Let's speculate for the moment as to why God might bring to the surface intercessors in the 1970s, prophets in the 1980s, and apostles in the 1990s in that particular sequence. I think the reason is clear. Intercessors needed to come first because their principal task is to clear the pathway in the invisible world between heaven and earth. They know how to use the spiritual authority that God has given them to bind and neutralize the demonic powers that strive to bring confusion. When they do their job well, the voice of God can be heard more clearly here on earth.

Who, then, are those most strongly anointed by God to hear His voice? Of course they are the prophets. With the intercessors in action, the prophets can hear from God more accurately and communicate that message to the body of Christ. However, and there are notable exceptions, prophets by and large can receive the correct message from God, but most of the time they have little or no idea as to what to do with it. That's where apostles come into the picture.

One of the major functions of apostles is to *"set in order the things that are lacking,"* as Paul wrote to Titus (Tit. 1:5). Apostles take the word of the Lord from prophets (they also, of course, hear from God directly as well); they judge it, they interpret it, they strategize their procedures, and they assume leadership in implementing it. For God's purposes to be fully realized, then, intercessors, prophets, and apostles are all needed, and in that sequence. Once they came into place, the stage was set for entering the Second Apostolic Age in 2001.

## Is This Biblical?

In case there may be some doubts, I want to pause to substantiate that the trends for the church I have been describing are biblical. If I couldn't do this, I would be among the first to head off in a different direction.

There is a considerable amount of biblical material on apostles and apostolic ministry in the New Testament. However, in order to simplify things I will choose only three scripture quotes. I am basing my comments on the assumption that we agree that the Bible is the word of God. If we do, these three scriptures should be enough to persuade any lingering doubters.

The first is Ephesians 4:11. It reads: "And [Jesus at His ascension] gave some to be apostles, some prophets, some evangelists, and some pastors and teachers." Most of our churches today have comfortably recognized the offices of evangelist, pastor, and teacher. But many of them become uncomfortable with the mention of contemporary offices of apostle and prophet. They may say they believe that the Bible is 100 percent inspired, but somehow they only seem to recognize 60 percent of this particular Bible verse. They, quite understandably, prefer to remain in their comfort zones.

The second scripture is Ephesians 2:20, "[The household of God, i.e., the church], having been built on the foundation of apostles and prophets, Jesus Christ Himself being the chief cornerstone." Jesus, of course, founded the church, but at His ascension He delegated the operational nuts and bolts for the future growth of the church to apostles and prophets. He remains as the cornerstone. The cornerstone is not the foundation, per se, but it is the unit that holds the foundation together. The foundation is apostles and prophets. It could be argued that churches without apostles and prophets rest on a faulty foundation.

The third Scripture is 1 Corinthians 12:28. First Corinthians 12 is the most detailed chapter in the Bible on the spiritual gifts that God gives to the body of Christ. This particular verse is the only one that puts spiritual gifts into numerical order: "And God has appointed these in the church: first apostles, second prophets, third teachers, after that miracles, then gifts of healings, helps, administrations, varieties of tongues." The numbering is not simply a random selection. Although it does not imply a hierarchy, it is clearly a divine order. Apostles are first and prophets are second. All the other gifts will function to their fullest potential only if they are properly related to apostles and prophets.

A few may attempt to discount these three scriptures on the supposition that apostles and prophets were needed only for the first few years of the church, and that subsequently, especially after the Bible was written, they ceased. The theological term for this is "cessationism," derived from the word "cease." However, this is a difficult position to sustain, especially in light of the time line given in Ephesians 4:13. All five offices listed in Ephesians 4:11, which were given for the equipping of the saints (Eph. 4:12), were deemed necessary for how long? *"Till we all come to the unity of the faith and of the knowledge of the Son of God, to a perfect man, to the measure of the stature of the fullness of Christ."* Very few people I know would claim that the church has arrived at this point. The logical conclusion, then, would be that we still need apostles and prophets as well as the other foundational offices.

## Why the Title?

Numerous individuals have said words to me like this: "I agree that we need apostolic ministry in our churches today, but why use the title? As long as apostles are functioning as apostles, the title doesn't matter."

Curiously, those who pose this question would not ordinarily use the same reasoning with the title "pastor." Most local churches would not be content if their leader would say something like, "I can function as your pastor, but please don't call me pastor." No! The title "pastor," or sometimes "Reverend," implies a certain recognized job description within the congregation, and a certain role in the community outside the congregation. Or the same with a seminary professor. Only an oddball would say, "I will function as a teacher, but please don't give me the title of Doctor." If we are comfortable with titles for pastor and teacher, why would we be uncomfortable with the title of apostle?

Jesus wasn't uncomfortable. He was the one who introduced the title "apostle" into New Testament life in the first place. We are told that on one occasion Jesus went apart to pray all night and the next morning He called all His disciples to a meeting. In the meeting, He chose twelve of the disciples to be His top leaders, and He commissioned them with the title "apostles" (see Luke 6:12-13). In the society of Jesus' day, "apostle" had important military and political innuendos, and Jesus adapted the term to indicate a specific role in the extension of the kingdom of God. Its basic root meaning in Greek (*apóstolos*) is one sent with an assignment. However not all those whom Jesus sent were apostles, such as the seventy of Luke 10. The twelve apostles were more than just sent, they were also given apostolic leadership authority that Jesus' other disciples did not have.

The title "apostle" carries through the rest of the New Testament. It appears 74 times as contrasted to "teacher" (14 times), "prophet" (8 times), "evangelist" (3 times), and "pastor" (3 times). The authors of the New Testament epistles identify themselves as "apostle" 11 times as contrasted to "servant" (5 times), "elder" (2 times), and "prisoner" (1 time). I list these numbers in an attempt to show that the current inhibitions that some Christian leaders harbor preventing them from using the title "apostle" are undoubtedly rooted more in cultural conditioning than in scriptural exegesis.

## What Is an Apostle?

What is an apostle? My working definition has been as follows: An apostle is a Christian leader gifted, taught, commissioned, and sent by God with the authority to establish the foundational government of the church within an assigned sphere of ministry by hearing what the Spirit is saying to the churches and by setting things in order accordingly for the expansion of the kingdom of God.

The most common kind of an apostle is one who has been assigned by God to oversee a number of churches. They form apostolic networks and they are frequently called "vertical apostles." My personal apostolic role is different. It has more to do with convening certain groups of leaders such as educators, prophets, deliverance ministers, and other apostles. I, then, function as a "horizontal apostle."

The chief distinguishing characteristic of an apostle is God-given authority. Paul says to the Corinthians that he is not ashamed to boast of the authority that God has given him (see 2 Cor. 10:8). However, he goes on to point out that God has only authorized him to use his apostolic authority in certain spheres, one of which includes the Corinthians (see 2 Cor. 10:13). Unfortunately, some immature apostles suppose that they are apostles to the whole church, rather than recognizing the limitations of their spheres. They need to follow Paul's example when he says to the Corinthians, *"If I am not an apostle to others, yet doubtless I am to you"* (1 Cor. 9:2).

## A New Wineskin

The phenomenon of the Second Apostolic Age is clearly a new wineskin in the unfolding of the history of the church. New wineskins are common. As the church of Jesus Christ has grown through the centuries, it has never grown exactly the same way. It grew one way in New Testament times, another way in the Roman Empire before Constantine, another way in the Roman Empire after Constantine, another way in the Middle Ages, another way in the time of the Reformation, another way in the era of European colonization, and another way after World War II, just to select a few broad slices of church history. Every one of these changes in the patterns of church growth required a new wineskin.

Jesus taught about wineskins in conjunction with one of the most radical changes in the Bible, that of moving from the Old Covenant to the New Covenant. On one occasion John the Baptist's disciples came to see Jesus because they were very upset. They were upset because they were so hungry. John the Baptist was making them fast all the time, while Jesus and His disciples were eating and drinking and enjoying life. They asked Jesus for an explanation.

Jesus, in Matthew 9:14-17, taught them something about the bride and the bridegroom, then about putting new patches on old garments. Finally He came to wineskins. In this context, John the Baptist represented the old wineskin of the Old Covenant and Jesus represented the new wineskin of the New Covenant. Jesus said, *"Nor do [people] put new wine into old wineskins, or else the wineskins break, the wine is spilled, and the wineskins are ruined"* (Matt. 9:17).

## Our Attitude Counts

Since the point that I am making is that those of us in the churches of the New Apostolic Reformation are now the new 21st century wineskin, I feel it is essential for us to display the correct attitude toward the old wineskins. Jesus did not despise either John the Baptist or the old wineskin. In fact, at one point He said there had been no man born of a woman greater than John (see Matt. 11:11). Every one of God's old wineskins, at one point in time, was once a new wineskin. The reason God does not pour His new wine into the old wineskins is based on His mercy. He does not want to ruin the old wineskins because He loves the old wineskins. In fact, old wine is typically treasured by wine connoisseurs.

The major ecclesiastical wineskin for the past few centuries has been denominations, and previous to that it was state churches. Even though we are in the Second Apostolic Age, denominations are not going to vaporize any more than the Jewish Old Covenant vaporized after Jesus came. Jesus comments on this when He says, *"No one, having drunk old wine, immediately desires new; for he says, 'The old is better'"* (Luke 5:39). However, while we continue to honor those who prefer the old wine, at the same time we are not reluctant to suggest that right now, if we want to be among God's history-changers in this new season, we would do well to be in the place where we can receive His new wine. *"But new wine must be poured into new wineskins"* (Luke 5:38).

## Looking at the New

What are some of the characteristics of the 21st century wineskins of the church? One is the name, the New Apostolic Reformation. "Reformation" denotes, as I have said, that we are now witnessing the most radical change in the way of doing church since the Protestant Reformation. In fact, I believe a reasonable argument could be made that the current change in doing church (not a change in basic theology) may be even greater than that of the Reformation.

The term "Apostolic" highlights the most radical of all the changes, namely the recognition of the office of apostle in the church today. There is a new acceptance of the fact that the Holy Spirit, in implementing God's design for the body of Christ, delegates extraordinary amounts of spiritual authority to individuals. The assumption in the old wineskin of denominations was that all final decisions must be made by church groups of one sort or another, and not entrusted to any one individual. In new apostolic churches, however, pastors turn out to be the leaders of the local church rather than employees of the church. And on the translocal level, apostles, rather than councils or synods or presbyteries or general assemblies or other such groups, are in charge. This allows what one leader terms "pain-free church government."

The word "new" is used to distinguish this movement from a number of denominations which are old wineskins, but which have included the word "apostolic" in their name. My observation is that many leaders are now dropping "New" and calling this movement simply the Apostolic Reformation.

The Apostolic Reformation displays many notable features other than pain-free church government. They initiated the contemporary worship style, which is now being adopted by a growing number of churches across the board. Outreach is a prominent part of their DNA with planting churches and sending missionaries and caring for the poor and needy built into their structure. Finances, across the board, are more plentiful. These churches teach tithing, as well as regularly giving offerings over and above the tithe, as essential to a life pleasing to God. The apostolic churches are vision-driven in contrast to their counterparts, which tend to be more heritage-driven.

Because the biblical role of apostles, prophets, evangelists, pastors, and teachers is to equip all of the saints for the work of the ministry (see Eph. 4:12), the congregation, rather than traditional Bible schools and theological seminaries, becomes the primary incubator for new church leaders. Strong pastors, not the church per se, employ their staff members and appoint elders who support them and their vision. They also assume the responsibility of selecting and training their successors in contrast to entrusting search committees with that responsibility. Quite frequently, the successor turns out to be the son of the senior pastor. Clergy couples, with both husband and wife as co-pastors, are more common than they were in the old wineskin.

## Demonstrations of Power

Since the genealogy of the New Apostolic Reformation traces back through the independent charismatic movement and classical Pentecostalism, it would be expected that demonstrations of the power of the Holy Spirit would be common. Not all apostolic churches would self-identify as charismatic in nature, but probably 80 percent would. I think, however, that nearly all would allow occasional sign gifts in their midst, but not necessarily as a part of their public ministry.

Having said that, most apostolic churches would like to have the reputation of identifying with the apostle Paul who said, *"And my speech and my preaching were not with persuasive words of human wisdom, but in demonstration of the Spirit and of power"* (1 Cor. 2:4). Their ongoing church life would include prophecy and tongues and concert prayer and exuberant body language and banners and dancing and healings and deliverance ministries and prophetic acts and proactive spiritual warfare and altar calls for personal prayer.

## Apostolic Ears

Seven times in the Book of Revelation Jesus says, "He who has an ear, let him hear what the Spirit says to the churches." His statement occurs in each of the letters to the seven churches in Revelation 2 and 3.

Every believer can and should hear what the Holy Spirit is saying. For example, you need to hear what the Spirit is saying about the direction of your life. A teacher needs to hear what the Spirit is saying about his or her class. A mayor needs to hear what the Spirit is saying to the city. A CEO needs to hear what the Spirit is saying to the business. A pastor needs to hear what the Spirit is saying to his or her church. But none of those are the ones whom God has principally appointed to hear what the Spirit is saying to the *churches* (plural).

It is the apostles properly related to prophets, more than anyone else, who need to have the ear to hear what the Spirit is saying to the churches. Vertical apostles who oversee 100 or 1,000 churches need to hear what the Spirit is saying to the churches in their network, but not all of them are responsible for hearing what the Spirit is saying to churches in general. Some apostles, however, are responsible for that, and they are the ones who have what I am calling "apostolic ears." Paul refers to them in Ephesians 3:5 when he speaks of revelation "which in other ages was not made known to the sons of men, as it has now been revealed by the Spirit to His holy apostles and prophets."

I decided to write this book on taking dominion because I have been hearing so many with apostolic ears saying that one of the highest items on God's current agenda for His people is social transformation. I have no doubt at all that this is what the Spirit is saying to the churches today. Furthermore, I believe that God did not speak so strongly about this before now because He knew that it was necessary to have the biblical government of the church in place before it could be properly implemented.

Social transformation is the battle cry for the Second Apostolic Age. The next chapter will explain what social transformation involves for all of us.

Chapter 2

# A NEW HORIZON: SOCIAL TRANSFORMATION

I can remember when not just a few of us evangelical leaders, but a whole lot of us would assume that a book on social transformation could be written only by a liberal. Momentarily, I want to explain the very interesting historical process that led us to that erroneous conclusion.

First, however, I would like to say that we are clearly in a new season. As I mentioned in the last chapter, the Holy Spirit has now begun to speak strongly to the churches about taking dominion or, in other words, transforming society. Now that we are in the Second Apostolic Age, we have in place a governmental infrastructure of the church much more capable of supporting an assignment to transform cities and nations and other social units than we have had before.

## The Hebrew Mindset

One of the most significant changes in this new wineskin is a distinct shift from what we could call the "Greek mindset" to the "Hebrew mindset." The Bible, both the Old Testament and the New Testament, comes out of the background of a Hebrew mindset. The basic idea behind the Hebrew mindset is that God and spiritual principles permeate all of life here on earth. Some people call it "holistic." True, the New Testament was written in the Roman Empire which had assimilated the Greek mindset, but, with the exception of Luke, it was written by Jews. However, as the church developed over the centuries, more and more of the Greco-Roman culture crept in until Emperor Constantine finally hijacked the church and, to all intents and purposes, completed the switch.

Bryant Myers, Professor of Transformational Development at Fuller Seminary, is one of the most accomplished theoretician-practitioners of the current social transformation movement. He calls it "transformational development." For years he has been on the forefront of trying to pull the church back into the Hebrew mindset. In his book *Walking with the Poor*, here is how he explains what has been happening.

Myers says:

> Throughout this book I will struggle to overcome problems presented by the persistent and insistent belief in the West [Myers is referencing the Greek mindset] that the spiritual and physical domains of life are separate and unrelated. This assumption has invaded and controlled almost every area of intellectual inquiry, including development theory and practice as well as much Christian theology. I will seek an understanding of development in

which physical, social, and spiritual development are seamlessly interrelated.[1]

This reflects the typical Hebrew approach to life.

## Christians Should Change the World

I agree with Bryant Myers, and clearly we are not the only ones who are thinking that way. Another is James Davidson Hunter, a sociologist from the University of Virginia. Look at this question that Hunter raises: "While Americans are among the most religious people on earth" (56 percent worship at least monthly, 43 percent weekly) "how is it that our culture is thoroughly secular?"[2] Most of us have heard questions like this numerous times, and, to be honest, answers have been hard to come up with. I believe that one of the causes of this is our Greek mindset, which tells us that Christians should be concerned with saving souls and going to heaven rather than paying much attention to material things like transforming our societies.

Hunter, to the contrary, says, "Most Christians in history have interpreted the creation mandate in Genesis as a mandate to change the world."[3] Consider what a radical suggestion this is. As I think back to my years and years of graduate theological training, I cannot remember hearing such a thing from any of my professors. I learned that, as Christian ministers, our assignment was to change people. The assumption was that if we got enough individuals saved, the world might then change. I find it significant that James Davidson Hunter is a sociologist, not a theologian.

Take Australia as an example. Not many Americans realize that Australia has been showing signs of significant social transformation, a good deal of which is attributed to a new upsurge of Christians taking seriously their mandate to change the world. Brian Pickering, head of the Australian Prayer Network, comments, "Not for many years have Christians had such an impact on a federal election. Not for many years has the Christian faith been the centre of national focus and discussion through all forms of the media...This election may come to be acknowledged as the turning point when personal faith took over from political correctness as the greatest influence upon the future direction of our society."[4]

As Christian believers, when we read something like this we want to applaud. It makes so much sense. Instead of letting society take its own course, why shouldn't we move out there, get our hands dirty, and change things for the good? We should! I believe that we will be seeing things like what happened in Australia all over the world because it is what the Spirit is currently saying to the churches. He will give us understanding and He will give us power to accomplish His purposes.

Speaking of understanding, if we're going to move in a new direction, we need to have a clear understanding of where we are at present. And one of the ways of knowing where we are now is to understand how we got here. Therefore, I think it will be very helpful at this point to paint some broad brush strokes across the canvas of social transformation history.

# Social Transformation History

## *Constantine*

Constantine became the emperor of Rome in the 4th century. As I mentioned earlier, the philosophical underpinnings of the Roman Empire had been molded by the Greek mindset. Famous thinkers of the past like Plato and Aristotle had shaped people's views of reality. They believed that reality had two overriding dimensions, the spiritual and the natural. The purest arena was the spiritual, the world of ideas. The natural or the material world was a necessary part of life, but an inferior arena. To the degree that people could absorb the spiritual and succeed in distancing themselves from the natural, the better off they would be.

This Greco-Roman perspective, sometimes known as "dualism," was different from God's original design for the world. He had no plans to separate the spiritual from the material, but rather to keep them both as integrated parts of the whole. What happens in the natural always affects the spiritual and vice versa. God's revelation, the Bible, is based on this presupposition that we have been calling the Hebrew mindset.

The church began in the Roman Empire among a small demographic unit, namely the Jews. While all of the first believers in Jesus the Messiah were Jews, the gospel soon began to spread to the Gentiles, and before long the Jews became a minority in the church. It was natural for the Jewish believers to see life through a Hebrew mindset, but for the Gentiles it required a paradigm shift. As the centuries leading to Constantine went by, predictably the prevailing Greco-Roman culture gained more and more of an influence over church leaders. Even though the Bible was birthed in Hebrew culture, it increasingly was interpreted and applied to the church through the dualistic ideas of the Greek mindset.

What does this have to do with social transformation? The surrounding culture influences the church. It always has and it always will. However, as we will see in detail in the next chapter, the church is part of the kingdom of God. Every culture, including the Greco-Roman culture, has been corrupted to one degree or another by the works of the enemy, and it is the duty of God's people to identify and change those ungodly aspects of culture so that God's kingdom comes on earth as it is in heaven.

Emperor Constantine professed conversion to Christianity. I say "professed," because only God knows if he was truly born again or if his actions were more of a political expedient than a spiritual experience. In any case, Constantine started a state church, making Christianity the official religion of the Roman Empire. At first this may seem like true social transformation, a victory for the kingdom of God. True, it did have some short-term benefits. For example, widespread persecution of the church became illegal, and as a result many more were born again. But long-range, it ended up producing negative effects, which we are still struggling with today.

Here's what happens with a state church. Instead of the church transforming the government, the government transforms the church. Under Constantine and his successors, the church became spiritually impotent and ended up in what we know as the Dark Ages. The church is called to influence the government, but not to rule over society. This is one reason why the threat of Muslim *sharia* law is so terrifying. We Christians learned our lesson through Constantine. As I detailed in the preface, we do not embrace a theocracy as a desired form of civil government.

## The Reformers

A huge change came with the Protestant Reformation of the 16th century. The two most outstanding leaders of the Reformation were Martin Luther of Germany and John Calvin of Geneva.

Martin Luther, the great reformer who broke the bondage of medieval Catholicism, laid the basic theological foundations of our Protestant movement with doctrines like the authority of Scripture, justification by faith, and the priesthood of all believers. All of us have benefited from his courageous and brilliant theological breakthroughs.

However, relating to our subject, Luther maintained the standard Greek-oriented dualism prevalent since Constantine. H. Richard Niebuhr, a recognized analyst of Luther's thought, says:[Luther] seems to have a double attitude toward reason and philosophy, toward business and trade, toward religious organizations and rites, as well as toward state and politics...Luther divided life into compartments, or taught that the Christian right hand should not know what a man's worldly left hand was doing.[5]

Luther himself was far from holistic. He said: There are two kingdoms, one the kingdom of God, the other a kingdom of the world...God's kingdom is a kingdom of grace and mercy...but the kingdom of the world is a kingdom of wrath and severity...Now he who would confuse these two kingdoms...would put wrath into God's kingdom and mercy into the world's kingdom, and that is the same as putting the devil in heaven and God in hell.[6] Luther was far from holistic.

I mention this because, in contrast, John Calvin, Luther's fellow reformer, had a more positive view of the mandate of the church to get involved with and transform culture. Neibuhr says:

> More than Luther [Calvin] looks for the present permeation of all life by the gospel. His more dynamic conception of the vocations of men as activities in which they may express their faith and love and may glorify God in their calling...leads to the thought that what the gospel promises and makes possible...is the transformation of mankind in all its nature and culture into a kingdom of God.[7]

A contemporary term for this position of John Calvin that I will refer to from time to time in this book is the "cultural mandate." By it I mean, simply, that we have an assignment from God to take dominion and transform society.

An example of how this cultural mandate played out in real life happened in Holland around 1900 through one of Calvin's disciples, Abraham Kuyper. Kuyper, an ordained Reformed minister and a renowned theologian, said that his deepest desire was:

In spite of all worldly opposition, God's holy ordinances shall be established again in the home,
in the school, and in the state for the good of the
people to carve, as it were, into the conscience of
the nation the ordinances of the Lord...until the
nation pays homage again to God.[8]

In order to make this happen, Kuyper ran for and was elected
Prime Minister of Holland. He truly brought social transformation to a nation.

But only for a time. It could be that one of the reasons
why Holland did not remain a transformed nation for long
was that Kuyper lacked insights into the strategic-level spiritual dimensions of social transformation. He did not explicitly
tune in to the proactive role that satan, along with the principalities and powers of darkness, played in infecting societies
with unrighteousness. For him, principalities and powers were
sinful human social institutions rather than demonic beings
per se. Because we are now correcting this, I have strong
hopes that we will see the kinds of social changes that Kuyper
brought sustained through succeeding generations.

## The U.S. Constitution and the Modern Missionary Movement

Neither Luther nor Calvin took steps to disband the
structures of the state church that Constantine instituted.
Both before and after the Reformation, it was assumed that
the government should be in charge of the church. Churches
like the Roman Catholic Church, the Lutheran Church, the
Reformed Church, the Anglican Church, and the Church

of Scotland (Presbyterian) were the only churches in their nations recognized and supported by the government. It seems strange to us today that pastors, for example, would be government employees, but such a thing commonly happens with state churches.

Parenthetically, it is important to note that a major reason why Abraham Kuyper could accomplish what he did was that his Dutch Reformed Church was the official state church of Holland at the time. That is one reason why today's strategies for social transformation will necessarily be different from Kuyper's.

The U.S. Constitution, ratified in 1783, and the Modern Missionary Movement pioneered by William Carey who went from England to India in 1792, fostered some of the first significant alternatives to state churches. The Constitution prohibited a state church in the United States. Also, when missionaries from state churches went to Hindu or Buddhist or Muslim or animistic nations, state churches were no longer possible. The result was the emergence of what we now know as denominations.

Faced with this new religious reality, the idea of transforming society began to take a back seat. Most people didn't know how to transform society without a state church. The missionary movement began to focus on what we call the "evangelistic mandate" to the exclusion of the cultural mandate. Winning souls and planting churches became the agreed upon central task. Improving the immediate social situation on the mission field by establishing schools and hospitals and orphanages and the like was common enough, but it was generally seen as a means toward saving more souls rather than as an effort to change the nation itself.

This focus on the evangelistic mandate also carried over to the great spiritual awakenings that have punctuated American history. Social reforms such as women's suffrage, abolition of slavery, and temperance were notable exceptions, not the rule. None of the awakenings themselves produced structural social transformation.

## The Social Gospel

In the late 1800s, the voice of Walter Rauschenbusch of Rochester, New York began to be heard. He attempted to bring the cultural mandate back to one of the front burners of the missionary movement alongside the evangelistic mandate. He is remembered today as one of the more prominent pioneers of what soon came to be called the Social Gospel Movement.

Unfortunately, it was at this point that the liberal element of the church succeeded in co-opting the cultural mandate. Ironically, Rauschenbusch himself advocated that the evangelistic mandate should be kept primary, but he wasn't able to stem the liberal tide. His Social Gospel followers alienated themselves from evangelicals by (1) attributing the root of social evil in the U.S. to capitalism, and (2) removing the evangelistic mandate from their agenda.

This caused a strong negative reaction among evangelical leaders as we moved into the 1900s. It helped provoke, among other things, the fundamentalist-modernist controversy. It caused evangelicals to reject the idea of social transformation because it became stereotyped as a liberal doctrine.

This is why I mentioned at the beginning of the chapter that there was a time when any book on social transformation, like this one, would have been assumed to be written by a liberal.

That, of course, has now changed. As best I can track it, the changes began in the 1960s. At that time, the Holy Spirit started speaking strongly to biblical, evangelical Christians about their responsibility to care for the poor and the oppressed. It seems like many of those who had ears to hear at the time were Latin American evangelical leaders. Unfortunately, some took the cultural mandate to an extreme and ended up with a flawed Latin American Theology of Liberation. Following in the footsteps of the U.S. Social Gospel, they appeared to regard the evangelistic mandate as a historical relic. Many liberal Latin American theologians seemed to be saying that the true message of the gospel was to save society from North American capitalism rather than to save souls and grow churches.

Back then, I was still serving as a field missionary in Latin America, I observed the trends first hand, and I was one of those who began to wave red flags. I decided to put my thoughts into a book, *Latin American Theology: Radical or Evangelical?* in order to warn others of this emerging liberalism. As soon as I did, I was blindsided by passionately negative reactions to my book on the part of some of my evangelical Latin American friends such as Samuel Escobar and René Padilla and Orlando Costas. I thought they would have agreed with my plea to keep the evangelistic mandate front and center. However, their main concern was that, to all intents and purposes, I was purposely neglecting the cultural mandate to transform society. Looking back, I now see that they were correct, although I must confess that at the time I proceeded to argue publicly and rather strenuously against them.

## Lausanne, 1974

The major turning point leading to where we are today was the International Congress on World Evangelization held in Lausanne, Switzerland in 1974. Sponsored by the Billy Graham Evangelistic Association and attended by 4,500 hand-picked delegates from virtually every nation of the world, the major focus was on the evangelistic mandate. However, enough people were there, including the Latin Americans I have mentioned, to bring the cultural mandate strongly to the attention of the Congress.

A controversy of sorts arose when the official position paper of the Congress, the Lausanne Covenant, was drafted. Much to the relief of my Latin American friends and others like them, the Lausanne Covenant included the cultural mandate. This was a decided break from the past. However, much to their disappointment, it stated that the evangelistic mandate was "primary." They wanted the two mandates to be placed on an equal plane, not one over the other. In fact, they were so passionate with their objections that they noisily refused to sign the Lausanne Covenant, deciding to draft their own counter-covenant, which they proceeded to sign instead.

It so happened that an ongoing body of 48 emerged from the congress called the Lausanne Committee for World Evangelization (LCWE), and I turned out to be one of the 48. My Latin American friends were not eligible because they had not signed the Lausanne Covenant. For the next 15 years, the course of LCWE was largely set by a Theology Working Group headed up by John Stott of the U.K. and a Strategy Working Group, which I headed up. While I was using my influence to keep the evangelistic mandate central, John Stott, who was the principal author of the Lausanne Covenant, was undergoing a paradigm shift, strongly swayed by my Latin American friends. Consequently, we found ourselves in an ongoing creative tension.

It is fascinating to me to review the public dialogue on issues related to social transformation that peaked during the 1980s, since (1) I was a key player and (2) I now see that I was on the wrong side. John Stott at one time before Lausanne had said, "The commission of the church is not to reform society, but to preach the Gospel."[9] Not long after that he began to change his position and he became an advocate of social transformation, just the opposite of where he was before. John Stott made this change probably twenty years before I finally did. Meanwhile, we convened two LCWE-related international meetings as platforms to air our differing views, one in Pattaya, Thailand (1980), and one in Grand Rapids, Michigan (1982).

Just for the record, here is the kind of thing I was saying at the time:

> From beginning to end [the Pattaya meeting] took
> a clear and direct stand on the issue of the primacy
> of evangelism...While recognizing that the cul-
> tural mandate is indeed part of holistic mission,
> [the meeting] refused to go the route of the World

Council of Churches and make it either primary or equal to evangelism.[10]

Now that I'm looking back, I can see that, regrettably, my influence and that of others like me persisted even to the Grand Rapids meeting, which was much more overtly oriented toward the cultural mandate than previous gatherings. The final paper said, among other things:

> Seldom if ever should we have to choose between satisfying physical hunger and spiritual hunger, or between healing bodies and saving souls, since authentic love for our neighbor will lead us to serve him or her as a whole person. Nevertheless, if we must choose, then we have to say that the supreme and ultimate need of all humankind is the saving grace of Jesus Christ, and that therefore a person's eternal, spiritual salvation is of greater importance than his or her temporal and material well-being.[11]

Over the years since then, the evangelical community has become more and more comfortable with the cultural mandate without fearing it would dilute the evangelistic mandate. By 2005, for example, the Mission America Coalition under Paul Cedar, which is the U.S. branch of LCWE, had begun to gear its programs toward transforming America, calling for cities to be renewed and redeemed. This was a departure from the past.

## Taking Our Cities for God, 1990

Meanwhile, the charismatically inclined evangelicals in the U.S. began to move in a direction somewhat different from traditional evangelicals by taking the biblical mandate for strategic-level spiritual warfare more seriously. Previous to 1990, not much had been written about, preached on, or discussed among leaders concerning high-ranking principalities and powers assigned by satan to keep whole segments of society in darkness and misery.

This began to change in the last large meeting of the Lausanne Movement, which took place in Manila in 1989. In Manila, no fewer than five of the international leaders who had been invited to speak chose to address the phenomenon of what came to be called "territorial spirits." I happened to be one of them. Before the meeting was over, I sensed the Lord prompting me to take a leadership role in communicating this concept to the body of Christ in general.

As I will detail in Chapter 6, a group of us subsequently formed a roundtable called Spiritual Warfare Network (SWN) to investigate issues concerning territorial spirits. One of the members of the SWN was John Dawson who had just published his landmark book, *Taking Our Cities for God*. In my opinion, it was his book, which sold 100,000 copies in 1990 alone, that firmly placed the cultural mandate on the agenda of charismatically inclined evangelicals. By expanding the plan of action from winning individuals to taking whole social units such as cities, Dawson initiated a major paradigm shift, which has grown stronger through the years. Taking action aimed at social transformation is no longer the exclusive domain of social-gospel liberals; those of us on the conservative end of the spectrum have now readjusted our priorities as well.

# "Social Transformation"

As more and more of the church begins to strategize along these lines, the sooner we can reach a general agreement on terminology the better we will be able to communicate with each other. I would like to argue that "social transformation," along with its derivatives, might be the most useful term. Some have been using "city taking" or "city reaching" or "transforming culture" or "renewal" or "restoration" or "reformation" or "redeeming the city." Each of these terms has merit, but they tend to scatter us instead of bringing us to a unified focus. With heavyweights like George Otis, Jr. (the Transformations series of videos), Luis Bush (Transform World), and Alistair Petrie (Transformed! People, Cities, Nations) using it, the term seems to be gaining wide acceptance. Once we agree that social transformation is a useful term, we must also agree on what we mean by it and how we measure it.

Luis Bush points out that the biblical word for transformation is derived from *metamorpho*, the word also used for a caterpillar being metamorphosed into a butterfly. Bush says, "Unlike reformation, [transformation] does not merely tinker with society; it changes it from inside out." He goes on to say:

> [Transformation] may be characterized by pervasive awareness of the reality of God, a radical correction of social ills, a commensurate decrease in crime rates, supernatural blessing on local commerce, healing of the brokenhearted (the alienated and disenfranchised), regenerative acts of

restoring the productivity of the land, and an exporting of kingdom righteousness.[12]

The analogy of the metamorphosis of a caterpillar into a butterfly also helps us come to realistic terms as to how to measure social transformation. The tendency over the past few years has been to use fuzzy measurements based mostly on anecdotes. Some lists of transformed cities or nations have reached into the hundreds. But what is meant by "transformed?" In most cases it means that the city is better off than it used to be. Some porn shops have closed or a school district has improved or a bank prays for its customers or the rate of AIDS has been reduced or wells have been dug or races have been reconciled or the economy has improved and on and on. I don't mean to trivialize any of the above, but I do not agree that any one of them, or even a cluster of a few of them, warrants using the past tense "transformed." Saying that certain cities are "in the process of transformation" would be much better.

I believe that our goal should be nothing short of *sociologically verifiable transformation*. By this I mean that an independent, outside, qualified observer, using standard tools of social science or investigative reporting, concludes that the social unit is now as different from what it used to be as a butterfly is from a caterpillar. Is this too high a standard? I don't think so. It seems to me that if we allow half-hearted, anecdotal measurements of transformation based largely on unprofessional enthusiasm, we put ourselves in danger of watering down the true message of the kingdom of God, which is for us to take dominion.

I agree with Ed Silvoso who affirms that "Nation transformation must be tangible, and the premier social indicator is the elimination of systemic poverty."[13] This is a radical suggestion, but it is both biblical and measureable. Poverty is a curse from satan, and *systemic* poverty means that babies who are born into certain social systems are destined to live lives of poverty. No matter what good things might happen, if systemic poverty still characterizes portions of a city or a region or a nation it should not be considered "transformed." Silvoso says that eliminating poverty is "the most tangible social evidence of true, biblically based transformation."[14]

## Almolonga, Guatemala

One of the best examples of sociologically verifiable transformation that we have to date is Almolonga, Guatemala. Almolonga was featured in George Otis Jr.'s first Transformations video, and since then it has become a popular Christian tourist attraction. Let's conclude this chapter by excerpting from a 2005 news release from CBN's Christian World News:

> Imagine a town where there are so few crimes the jails have been closed, and the food crops are so big and luscious they could have come from the Garden of Eden...The majority of Almolonga's 18,000 residents are farmers...On a typical market day, during one of the 8 harvests per year, tons and tons of fresh vegetables are gathered in the town center for export. Here they are loaded onto large tractor-trailers. An average of 40 of these tractor-trailers a day leave Almolonga,

loaded with some of the finest produce grown in the Western Hemisphere...The trailers that haul away vegetables are most often pulled by Mercedes Benz trucks.

It's been estimated that over 90% of Almolonga's people are now born again Christians...A generation ago, there were only 4 churches here. Today there are 23!

Pastor Harold Caballeros of El Shaddai Church in Guatemala City says repentance and revival have completely transformed Almolonga! Pastor Harold explained, "The mentality and the way of thinking of the people has changed so drastically! Changed from a culture of death, a culture of alcoholism, idolatry and witchcraft, to a culture today where they think only about expanding the kingdom of God—prosperity, blessing, healing."[15]

Social transformation? Yes, it can really happen through the power of God!

# Chapter 3

# A NEW PARADIGM: DOMINION THEOLOGY

If social transformation is what the Spirit seems to be saying to the churches today, we would expect that the Bible would support such an idea. Many will be asking the inevitable question: Is there a biblical theology to substantiate what we have been looking at up to this point?

Let's think about theology itself for a few moments.

## From Theoretical to Practical

I know that theology can be dull and boring. A reason for this is that much traditional theology, brilliant scholarship that it might be, finds very little intersection with practical reality. I suspect that we are seeing a subtle paradigm shift in the attitudes of many Christian leaders toward theology. Back when I went to seminary, practically the whole church was laboring under the assumption that a prerequisite for ordination was thorough instruction in systematic theology, epistemology, and the history of dogma. A rationale for this was that such expertise would be necessary for the church to avoid heresy. Ironically, however, it has become evident that some of the most damaging heresies currently plaguing the churches, at least in Europe and North America, have been perpetrated by none other than learned theologians.

I don't find the same level of reverence for theology in most churches associated with the New Apostolic Reformation. Take, for example, the school that I founded several years ago, Wagner Leadership Institute (WLI). Since WLI was designed to train adults who are already in ministry, I, for one thing, decided not to have any required courses in the curriculum. My thought was that the mature students whom we were teaching would know better what they needed for improving their own ministry than some faculty committee might surmise. One of the realities of this new tailored approach that quickly came to our attention was that if we offered traditional courses in systematic theology, epistemology, or the history of dogma, practically no one would sign up for them.

I'll go one step further and predict that theologians per se will likely become relics of the past as the Second Apostolic Age progresses. The Catholic Church has officially recognized the office of theologian and the Protestant equivalent is seminary professors whose courses, by the way, are, by necessity, required for graduation. New Apostolic churches, on the other hand, do not seem to be following in these footsteps. Their leaders do not seem to be carrying the excessive amount of doctrinal baggage that many of their predecessors did. Theologians are not mentioned, for example, in Ephesians 4:11 alongside apostles, prophets, evangelists, pastors, and teachers. All this does not imply an absence of sound theology, however. It is just that apostles, prophets, and teachers are becoming the new custodians of a dynamic theology that turns out to be just as much practical as theoretical.

## What Is Theology?

What are we talking about? What is theology anyway? Here is my attempt at a definition: Theology is a human attempt to explain God's word and God's works in a reasonable and systematic way. This is not a traditional definition. For one thing, it considers God's works as one valid source of theological information. For another, it sees God's word as both what is written in the Bible (logos) as well as what God is currently revealing (rhema). Admittedly, a downside of seeing theology in this way is possible subjectivity, but the upside is more relevance to what the Spirit is currently saying to the churches on a practical level. Teachers research and expound the logos, prophets bring the rhema, and apostles put it together and point the direction into the future.

## Dominion Theology

The practical theology that best builds a foundation under social transformation is dominion theology, sometimes called "kingdom now." Its history can be traced back through R.J. Rushdoony and Abraham Kuyper to John Calvin. Some of the pioneering attempts to apply it in our day would be notably Bob Weiner, Rice Broocks, Dennis Peacocke and others. Unfortunately, the term "dominion theology" has had to navigate some rough waters in the recent past. I think I understand where some of these objections have originated.

One objection, for example, comes from those who still hold the primacy of the evangelistic mandate over the cultural mandate. I explained the history of this creative dialogue very carefully in the last chapter, including my own former point of view that the evangelistic mandate was primary. Because I held that point of view myself, I believe I understand and respect the point of view of those who still object on these grounds.

## The End Times

A second objection is eschatological, dealing with our views of the end times. Dominion theology, true enough, tends to be eschatologically disruptive. Why? Many in my generation have been indoctrinated with the so-called "pre-trib, pre-mil" view of the end times. I cut my Christian teeth on the Scofield Bible and sat under those like Wilbur M. Smith who taught that the world was supposed to get worse and worse until finally all true believers would one day be raptured into heaven. Then those who had been left behind would go through seven years of tribulation with the antichrist gaining control until Jesus would return on a white horse and lead us all into one thousand years (a millennium) of reigning with Him. This was our glorious hope.

If, on the other hand, we now believe that God is mandating us to be involved in aggressive social transformation, it is obvious that we will arrive at a different viewpoint. We no longer accept the idea that society will get worse and worse because we now believe that God's mandate is to transform society so that it gets better and better. I agree with Jim Hodges who suggests that we Christians need to get rid of "our excessive desire to leave the planet."[1] This makes us much less dogmatic on theories of the millennium. I often say facetiously that I no longer know if I'm premillennial or postmillennial or amillennial. I've decided to be "panmillennial," believing that everything is going to "pan out" all right in the end!

Seriously, I will confess that up until recently I knew what eschatology I did *not* believe, namely the traditional *Left Behind* futuristic view, but I was not able to verbalize what I actually *did* believe. My changing point came when I read *Victorious Eschatology* by Harold Eberle and Martin Trench. Victorious eschatology fits dominion theology like a hand in a glove. Eberle and Trench say, "Before Jesus returns, the Church will rise in glory, unity, and maturity. The Kingdom of God will grow and advance until it fills the Earth."[2]

Victorious eschatology makes a convincing argument that many of the biblical prophecies concerning the "last days" or the "end times" were literally fulfilled in AD 70 at the time of the destruction of Jerusalem. The end times marked the ending of the Old Covenant and the beginning of the New Covenant. Jesus will literally return to the earth in the future (see Matt. 24:35-25:46), but none of the signs of Matthew 24:4-34 will precede His return because they have already occurred. This is known by professional theologians as the Partial Preterist view of eschatology, and it is the view with which I personally identify.[3]

## Crossing Boundaries

For some, however, this steps outside of strict traditional doctrinal boundaries. As an example, a prestigious denomination such as the Assemblies of God is committed to premillennialism, and this has predictably led them to oppose dominion theology. In one of their official publications, they list dominion theology under a series of "Deviant Teachings [Which Are] Disapproved" by the denomination's General Presbytery.[4]

A similar objection came from John Stott who, in his commentary on the Lausanne Covenant, wrote: What exactly is the church's expectation or hope? Some speak nowadays as if we should expect the world to get better and better, as if to secure conditions of material prosperity, international peace, social justice, political freedom, and personal fulfillment is equivalent to establishing the kingdom of God.... But Jesus gave no expectation that everything would get steadily better...This is simply not the Christian hope according to Scripture.[5]

I regret having to bring up a third objection that raised some barriers to the more general affirmation of dominion theology for a time, but it happens to be a fact that some of the higher-visibility and most vocal advocates of dominion theology unfortunately became subject to serious accusations of moral turpitude. While it would be difficult to draw any cause-and-effect conclusions from this, nevertheless many were understandably alienated from dominion theology because of this unsavory association.

# A New Season

So much for the rough waters that advocates of dominion theology had to navigate for a season. I am convinced that we are now in a new season. Growing numbers of church leaders are no longer shying away from the challenge of transforming society according to the values of the kingdom of God. The rough waters are becoming smoother.

Admittedly, this is a personal opinion, but I think the best way to proceed is to affirm and redeem the term "dominion theology," not to discard it. The most frequently suggested alternative is "kingdom theology." "Kingdom theology" is good, but I regard "dominion theology" as stronger, more action-based, more aggressive, and more biblically comprehensive. "Kingdom theology" tends to have pastoral connotations, while "dominion theology" leans more toward the apostolic. This is not to deny that the kingdom of God is the theological underpinning of dominion theology. Our prayer still must be "Your kingdom come, Your will be done on earth as it is in heaven."

# Genesis 1

The nuts and bolts of dominion theology begin in the first chapter of the Bible. The original stated intention of God was to create the human race so that they would *have dominion over the fish of the sea, over the birds of the air, and over the cattle, over all the earth and over every creeping thing that creeps on the earth*" (Gen. 1:26). This is the reason that I said I think "dominion theology" is more biblically comprehensive than "kingdom theology." The kingdom of God is a New Testament theme, while dominion is both Old Testament and New Testament.

The first thing that God said to Adam and Eve was, *"Be fruitful and multiply; fill the earth and subdue it; have dominion over [all the creation]"* (Gen. 1:28). We must not miss the significance of this statement. God not only created the earth, but He established a government for the earth with humankind, beginning with Adam and Eve, as the governors. He gave Adam and Eve full authority to take dominion in His name. But they were not puppets; they were free moral agents. What does this mean? This means that they had a choice. God would not coerce them. On the one hand they could take dominion, but on the other hand they had the authority to give their dominion away.

We often miss this point, mainly because we think we know the creation story so well. Chapter 2 gives us some additional details of the creation without mentioning dominion. By the time the serpent appears in Chapter 3, we might well have forgotten about dominion, which would be a mistake because that was what satan was essentially after. Our traditional interpretation is that satan wanted to break Adam and Eve's relationship with God and thereby introduce original sin, which would then be transmitted genetically to all their human progeny through the ages so that people would not go to heaven but to hell. That was certainly one of satan's goals, but an even greater one was to usurp the dominion over the world that God had given to Adam.

# Power and Authority

Before his fall in heaven, satan, or lucifer, had both power and authority. He was called *"the anointed cherub who covers"* (Ezek. 28:14). His big mistake was to say one day, *"I will ascend into heaven, I will exalt my throne above the stars of God"* (Isa. 14:13). He was not satisfied with authority delegated by God; he wanted to assert his own authority above God's. He said, *"I will be like the Most High"* (Isa. 14:14). As a result, he was cast down. When he was, he did not lose his power, but he did lose his authority. Then when God delegated authority for dominion over the creation to Adam, along with free moral choice, satan saw an opportunity to take back the authority he had lost. God would not have given it back to him, but Adam now could.

This may sound strange at first, but think about it. God had given Adam the authority to give his authority over to satan! This throws quite a different light on our usual understanding of the temptation and fall.

The so-called "apple" became simply the visual symbol of Adam's choice. Would he choose to obey God or would he go satan's way? When satan convinced him to disobey God, history was suddenly changed. Adam's authority to take dominion over God's creation was passed over to satan. Worse yet, Adam put himself and the whole future human race under the authority of satan as well.

## A "Toothless Lion?"

Check human history out. Think of some of the biblical terminology to describe satan and his dominion. He is *"the prince of the power of the air"* (Eph. 2:2). He is *"the god of this age" (2 Cor. 4:4). He is "the ruler of this world"* (John 14:30). These awesome titles are not to be taken lightly. Some insecure preachers who pooh-pooh satan's power by calling him a "toothless lion" need a reality check. The first step toward defeating an enemy is to gain a realistic appraisal of who the enemy really is.

Think of the miserable condition of the human race before Jesus came. Think of the lawlessness, the atrocities, the bloodshed, the oppression, the immorality, the idolatry, the witchcraft, the wars, and the disease that characterized whole peoples in all parts of the world. Think of the Ayoré Indian mothers of the Bolivian jungles who routinely buried alive their first born. Think of the Aztec altars running 24/7 with a fresh stream of blood from virgins who were being sacrificed to demonic forces. Yes, there were godly exceptions like Job and Noah and repentant Nineveh and the Israelites for certain seasons when God was being glorified. But these exceptions were few and far between compared to the bulk of the whole human race, which was under the dominion of satan, which he had usurped from Adam. No toothless lion there! Ask one of the Aztec virgins!

Paul's view of humanity is very realistic.

> *And you He made alive, who were dead in trespasses and sins, in which you once walked according to*

*the course of this world, according to the prince of the power of the air, the spirit who now works in the sons of disobedience, among whom also we all once conducted ourselves in the lusts of our flesh, fulfilling the desires of the flesh and of the mind, and were by nature children of wrath, just as the others* (Ephesians 2:1-3).

A fresh look at Jesus' temptation will remove any lingering doubts that satan had acquired true dominion over the earth. What I am going to say now assumes that we believe the three temptations were real. They were literal, not just figurative. In each of the three, Jesus could have decided to sin, which, of course, He didn't. So let's look at the third temptation when *"the devil took Him up on an exceedingly high mountain, and showed Him all the kingdoms of the world and their glory"* (Matt. 4:8). How many kingdoms? *All* the kingdoms of the world! Then satan said, *"All these things I will give You if You will fall down and worship me"* (Matt. 4:9). If the temptation was real, satan must have had the authority over the kingdoms in order to make this offer. Even though Jesus did not yield to the temptation, He never questioned the devil's authority over the kingdoms.

## The Second and Last Adam

If God's plan for history suddenly changed with the first Adam in the Garden of Eden, it just as suddenly changed back with the coming of the second and last Adam, Jesus Christ. We hear relatively little preaching on Jesus as the second Adam mainly because most Christian leaders have not been strongly tuned in to the dominion theology that I have been advocating. Once we become tuned in, however, what Paul writes in 1 Corinthians 15 becomes extremely relevant:

> *"The first man Adam became a living being." The last Adam became a life-giving spirit. ...The first man was of the earth, made of dust; the second Man is the Lord from heaven* (1 Corinthians 15:45,47).

Most preaching, like that of Billy Graham for example, highlights the pastoral dimension of Jesus' death on the cross. He died for our personal sins in order to reconcile us individually to God. Theologians call this the "substitutionary atonement." Through Jesus we can become saved, born again, new creatures in Christ, holy, saints of God, and whatever else is necessary to fulfill the destiny for which God put each of us on the earth as individuals and ultimately to end up in heaven. This is so important that many of us can even remember the day on which we first decided to commit our lives to Jesus Christ as Lord and Savior.

Beyond that, however, there is also what I like to think of as an apostolic dimension to Jesus' death on the cross. Here is the way that Joseph Mattera puts it: "The main purpose of Jesus dying on the cross was not so that you can go to heaven. The main purpose of His death was so that His kingdom can be established in you so that, as a result, you can exercise kingdom authority on the earth (Luke 17:21) and reconcile the world back unto Him (2 Cor. 5:19)."[6] Mattera obviously is not denying the pastoral dimension; he is simply affirming that there is much more to Christ's death than that. He is dealing with dominion.

# The Works of the Devil

God sent Jesus in true human flesh to do what Adam failed to do. Jesus lived a human life of purity and obedience to the Father. He was the only human being who ever lived who qualified to take back the dominion from satan that Adam had lost. *"For this purpose the Son of God was manifested, that He might destroy the works of the devil"* (1 John 3:8). The major works of the devil were wrapped up in the evil and tyrannical dominion that satan had exercised over the whole human race since the first Adam's fall. Jesus died to reverse history once and for all.

Look why the Father sent Jesus: *"For it pleased the Father that in Him all the fullness should dwell, and by Him to reconcile all things to Himself, by Him, whether things on earth or things in heaven, having made peace through the blood of His cross"* (Col. 1:19-20). How is this supposed to happen in real life? *"[God] has given us the ministry of reconciliation"* (2 Cor. 5:18). This becomes quite a responsibility! For whom? For those of us who are committed to do God's will. Among other things, it is a mandate for social transformation.

Joseph Mattera agrees. He says, "When Jesus was crowned Lord of all, it was over God's entire jurisdiction—not just the church—and this includes 'all things.' All 'things' include the land, the environment, politics, education, science, medicine, healthcare, the arts, space, economics, social justice and all the humanities."[7]

# That Which Was Lost

At one point, here is how Jesus described His own mission: *"For the Son of Man has come to seek and to save that which was lost"* (Luke 19:10). Our traditional pastoral understanding of this statement has been that Jesus came to save "those" who were lost, not "that" which was lost. Of course, He did come to save individual souls, as I have said, but this particular verse does not refer to individuals; it refers to the dominion over creation that Adam lost in the Garden of Eden. I like the way Ed Silvoso explains this: "Many Christians have no trouble believing that the devil—a created being with limited power—contaminated all creation with just one sin. But they find it difficult to believe that Jesus Christ—who is God— through a perfect sacrifice has made provision to recover all of 'that which was lost.'"[8] Silvoso adds the apostolic dimension.

Jesus' public ministry began right after His temptation. One of the first things that He did in His public ministry was to go into the synagogue in His hometown of Nazareth. There He delivered what was very likely His first public address. Not surprisingly, He used this occasion to lay out His ministry agenda. Here it is, taken from the Book of Isaiah:

> *The Spirit of the Lord is upon Me, because He has anointed Me to preach the gospel to the poor; He has sent Me to heal the brokenhearted, to proclaim liberty to the captives and recovery of sight to the blind, to set at liberty those who are oppressed; to proclaim the acceptable year of the Lord* (Luke 4:18-19).

This is the gospel of the kingdom. It is clearly a blending of the cultural mandate with the evangelistic mandate.

## Colonization

Speaking of the gospel of the kingdom, Myles Munroe suggests that God's plan for the earth could be seen as a form of what we know as colonization. "Colonization," Munroe says, "is a process whereby a government or ruler determines to extend his kingdom, rulership, or influence to additional territory with the purpose of impacting that territory with his will and desires."[9] God's reign was in the heavenlies, and He created the earth with the thought of extending His reign. Earth was to be a colony of heaven. God was the king of all, and He delegated the human race, represented in the beginning by Adam, to be the governors over this colony. The visible earth is supposed to reflect the nature and the essence of the invisible parent kingdom of heaven. Jesus' announcement in the synagogue of Nazareth was a declaration that this original intent of God would, from then on, begin to materialize in its fullness.

The second Adam did all that was necessary to put back in place God's original design for the earth as a colony of heaven. Once He did, He then delegated the responsibility of bringing God's plan into being. Steve Thompson says:

> Jesus, having won back authority on earth, could now mediate and rule in the affairs of earth. However, Jesus did not stay on the earth to rule it. He ascended to the Father and is seated at His right

hand. So who is now responsible to rule and reign in the earth? Believe it or not, the church, which is the body of Christ.[10]

This thought should move us from a passive mode to an active mode. A good part of the church expects that if we just pray enough for social transformation, God in His omnipotence will transform it. I don't think so. God expects us to pray, but He also wants to give us the authority and the resources and the revelation to move out in the power of the Holy Spirit and take back dominion from satan.

One thing that should help is for us to begin to shift our focus from redeeming individuals to redeeming society as our end goal. Don't get me wrong. This is not to deny that the more individuals saved the better. Let's do whatever is necessary to save more! But it is to suggest that just saving individuals will not necessarily lead to social transformation. Joe Woodard reports an interesting debate between sociologist James Davidson Hunter and Chuck Colson of Prison Ministry on this subject. Colson favors the grassroots individual approach assuming that "transformed people transform cultures."[11]

Hunter said that "cultures never change from the bottom up, but from the top down.[12]

The best strategy, according to Hunter, would be to aim directly for the institutions that mold culture. As well as praying for individuals to be saved, let's also pray for redeeming entire social institutions.

# The Great Commission

Although I am a bit reluctant to suggest it, I am convinced that we need to take a closer look at the Great Commission. We need to come to grips with what Jesus meant when he commanded His followers to *"make disciples of all the nations"* (Matt. 28:19).

The reason I am reluctant to bring this up is because for most of my career as a missiologist specializing in the Great Commission I confess that I advocated the individualistic approach. I refused to interpret "all the nations" as social units, even though that would be the literal translation of *panta ta ethne.* I leaned toward Chuck Colson's assumptions and taught that the only way the social units embraced by the term *ethne,* from which we get the English "ethnic groups," could be discipled would be to win enough souls to Christ within each *ethnos,* baptize them, and get them into local churches, and assume that they would provide the salt and light necessary for change.

This is now especially embarrassing because my missiological mentor, Donald McGavran, always interpreted the Great Commission as a mandate to change the whole social unit. McGavran said:

> According to the Great Commission the peoples are to be discipled. Negatively, a people is discipled when the claim of polytheism, idolatry, fetishism or any other man-made religion on its corporate loyalty is eliminated. Positively, a people is discipled when its individuals feel united around Jesus

Christ as Lord and Saviour, believe themselves to me members of His Church, and realize that "our folk are Christians, our book is the Bible, and our house of worship is the church." Such a reorientation of the social organism [emphasis mine] around the Lord Jesus Christ will be accompanied by some and followed by other ethical changes.[13]

As the first incumbent of the Donald McGavran Chair of Church Growth at Fuller Seminary, I knowingly became a McGavran revisionist at that point. One of the first things I now want to do when I get to heaven is to find McGavran and apologize! Without using the term, he was inherently convinced that we should take dominion, and I now agree.

Acts 3:21 talks of Jesus being in heaven "until the times of restoration of all things, which God has spoken by the mouth of all His holy prophets since the world began." "Restoration" also means transformation, and this dates back to the beginning when Adam and Eve were in the Garden of Eden. Even though Jesus came and changed history, He is waiting for us to do our part in bringing restoration to pass in real life. Meanwhile, He is reigning through us until *He puts an end to all rule and all authority and power. For He must reign till He has put all enemies under His feet"* (1 Cor. 15:24-25).

It is our task to become spiritual and social activists until satan's dominion is ended.

# Chapter 4

# A NEW THEOLOGICAL BREAKTHROUGH: GOD HAS AN OPEN MIND

Here is a question for thought. Does what we do really matter?

For example, I ended the last chapter with these words: "It is our task to become spiritual and social activists until satan's dominion is ended." Suppose we all responded, "No! I don't want to do that!" Would that choice make any difference? Couldn't God just go ahead and transform society without us? After all, isn't God all-powerful? Can't He do anything He wants? If He doesn't like satan and what satan does, why doesn't He wipe him off the face of the earth? Wouldn't we all be better off without the devil around anymore?

If we think about these questions for a moment or two, we realize that they are not idle questions. As a matter of fact, the best of Christian theologians have wrestled with these questions and others that spin off from them for centuries and centuries. Go to the library in any theological seminary and you will find shelves of books by learned authors who take such things very seriously.

## Kingdom Action

This is a book on taking dominion. I strongly believe that kingdom action on the part of all believers can literally change the world. John Wesley reportedly said words to this effect: "In prayer I learned that without God I cannot and without me God will not." This is a profound statement. Wesley seems to be saying that what we do really matters. It not only matters to the world and to those around us, but it also matters to God. God's plans, according to this point of view, apparently are not all set in concrete. The all-powerful or omnipotent God will use His power in one way if we do certain things and He will use it in another way if we don't. The outcome of certain human efforts will not hinge on whether God has or doesn't have power. Surprisingly enough, it will hinge on the choices that He allows us believers to make.

What I have just said is very controversial. It is what theologians have written all those books about. In a moment I'll explain some details of the rather hot debate that is going on right now in Christian leadership circles on what some call the "openness of God." But up front I want to make it clear that, after serious and lengthy consideration, for better or for worse, I personally have come to a conclusion and formed an opinion. My opinion is that what is known as "open theism" provides us the most biblical and the most helpful theological framework for doing our part in seeing "Your kingdom come, Your will be done on earth as it is in heaven."

In this chapter, with all due respect to those who might differ from me, I want to argue my case the best I can. As I do, I also want to be humble enough to admit up front that I may be wrong, although obviously I don't think that I am. The issues at stake are not those that threaten the validity of Christianity or those that could be labeled "heresy" or those that question the authority of scripture. They are simply respectable theological differences of opinion.

## The Garden of Eden

When I argued my case for dominion theology in the last chapter I began in the Garden of Eden. Let's do the same for open theism.

God's clear and stated purpose for creating Adam and Eve on the sixth day, after He had created everything else on the first five days, was as follows: *"Let Us make man in Our image, according to Our likeness; let them have dominion over the fish of the sea, over the birds of the air, and over the cattle, over all the earth and over every creeping thing that creeps on the earth"* (Gen. 1:26).

If God wanted to, He could have done it differently. He could have created Adam and Eve with the authority to take dominion, as He did. But He could also have kept satan, the serpent, out of the garden, and He could have allowed history to develop happily under the oversight of the sinless human race forever. Why didn't He do it that way? The issue was control. God did not want to use His power to coerce Adam to do anything. Adam was intentionally created a free moral agent. God wanted Adam to love Him, but true love has to be the choice of the individual. True love is never forced. That's why the choice was up to Adam. He could choose to go God's way or he could choose to go satan's way.

Adam, as we well know, made a bad choice. But let's shift our focus for a moment from Adam to God. What was God's role in this choice? Did God make Adam do what he did? Did God create Adam in order that he would sin so that God could eventually send a Redeemer? Did God know before He created him that Adam would not choose to love Him, but rather yield to satan? Did God create Adam to take dominion over creation knowing that, within a short period of time, satan would usurp that dominion and become the god of this age? Did God consciously create the human race while knowing that the great majority of the people He made in His image would end up in hell instead of in heaven?

## Heavy Questions

I know that these are heavy thoughts. They are not the usual topics of conversation in Starbucks. Most people would rather not care to even raise such questions about God, to say nothing of trying to answer them. But I don't believe we should pretend that they do not exist. After a bit of thought, most common believers whom I know and minister with would answer "no" to each of the questions in the last paragraph, although they might also admit that they would not be prepared to have to explain exactly how they came to their conclusions. The ones who would hedge their answers and try to give some logical explanations as to why God would create a world that He already knew would end up a disaster generally would be those who have had some formal theological train-ing. Almost all of them would be answering those questions out of a theological paradigm called "classical theism." I'm very familiar with classical theism, by the way, because that is what I learned and tried to believe when I took my graduate theological training.

If I may be personal for a moment, I will not forget my frustration over these issues during my first year in seminary. I lived in a house with about twenty other students and I've lost count of the number of nights that we would drink coffee together and stay up until 2:00 AM with the sole purpose of trying to figure out the final, definitive answers to these ques-tions about God, mainly because we were not entirely happy with the answers that our theological professors were propos-ing in class. Our professors were attempting to explain clas-sical theism to us. We learned enough to pass the exams, but our frustration was that what we learned did not always seem to line up very well with reality.

Our underlying problem, now that I look back, was that we had been given no theological alternatives. We were taught that God was sovereign, that he was infinite, eternal, omni-scient, omnipotent, and omnipresent, that He was unchange-able, and that He was just. We learned about predestination and foreknowledge and irresistible grace and limited atone-ment. The school was intentionally indoctrinating us with "Reformed Theology," dating back largely to John Calvin, one of the famous European reformers of the 16th century. Yes, we were told that there were attempts other than Calvin-ism to answer those tough questions, such as Pelagianism and

Arminianism, but they were considered at worst heretical or at best foolish and unsophisticated.

When I finished my studies and went to Bolivia as a field missionary, my escape from this theological frustration was simply to ignore the questions. If I couldn't come to reasonable answers in three years of seminary, I concluded that I probably never would. I did ministry on the assumption that what I was doing really mattered, but I couldn't explain the theology behind my actions very well.

## Open Theism

My frustrations ended in the late 1990s when I first heard about open theism. I began reading Greg Boyd and Clark Pinnock and John Sanders, probably the three highest profile advocates of open theism. It felt like I was being theologically born again. I finally had a biblical and theological paradigm that made sense of what I had been thinking and what I had been doing all along.

What was different between classical theism and open theism? It was a different understanding of God. Classical theism had led me to believe that because God was sovereign, He had all things under control. He was all-powerful. He had predetermined and He knew ahead of time everything that would ever happen in history. It was impossible for God not to know everything ahead of time. Nothing ever took God by surprise. Whatever happened through the ages must somehow fit into His overall design. Even though He didn't like evil, in the long range everything that took place, both good and bad, ultimately glorified God. This is why He could create

Adam and Eve while knowing all the while that they would end up sinning and transferring the authority that God had given them to take dominion over to satan. Can you see why I was frustrated? This line of thinking can end up forcing us to believe that what we do doesn't really matter very much. God has it all figured out ahead of time, and it will happen no matter what.

## How Free Is God?

Open theism provides another way of thinking about God. Like classical theism, it starts out with a clear biblical understanding that God is sovereign. That means that, among other things, He is all-powerful and that He can do whatever He wants. Both sides agree on this. God's sovereignty is non-negotiable. But open theism suggests that, while God decided ahead of time that certain things would happen no matter what, He also decided to leave some other things open and depending on the choices that human beings would make. Not only that, but consider this: Isn't God sovereign enough to limit His own sovereignty if He wants to?

Why might God wish to limit His own sovereignty? Simply put, to maintain His integrity. If God decides to leave certain things in history depending on our human decisions, it would not seem right if He knew ahead of time what our decisions would be. It would be like setting the slot machines in a gambling casino. It only makes sense that in certain situations, God would decide not only to keep things open, but even to choose to prevent Himself from knowing ahead of time what choices we would make.

Take, for example, Adam and Eve in the garden. Could it be that God chose not to know what decision they would make ahead of time? If so, His Plan A clearly was that they would have dominion, but because of Adam's bad choice God then decided to go to Plan B. He didn't create Adam specifically for Plan B, which is where he ended up.

Think about the other point of view. It argues that God actually knew what Adam's decision would be before he made it. In that case, God would have been saying something like this to Himself, "I know that Adam is going to eat the apple, but I'm going to tell him not to eat it anyway." For some, this could be a troubling view of God.

## The Evangelical Theological Society

What I have just said is very upsetting to those who have been programmed with classical theism and who do not intend to change. In fact, some of them would go so far as to say that open theism is an outright heresy. This is precisely what happened in the prestigious Evangelical Theological Society to which a majority of recognized, credentialed, Bible-believing, evangelical theologians belong. It is a fascinating story.

Everything had been going along pretty calmly in the Evangelical Theological Society (ETS) for years. Theologians, true to form, found plenty of things to debate about, but their debates weren't overly exciting and the issues were not particularly important. Until open theism came along! Then things blew wide open because the majority of ETS members happened to be committed classical theists.

The three outstanding proponents of open theism, Greg Boyd, Clark Pinnock, and John Sanders, began writing books and articles arguing their position. It is notable that all three were considered by their peers as respectable theologians, meaning that their theological arguments could not be ignored or swept under the carpet. All were members of ETS, even though Greg Boyd resigned in the early stages of the debate because God was leading him out of academia and into the pastorate. Pinnock and Sanders remained as members.

The issue was brought to its first Evangelical Theological Society vote by the classical theists in 2001. They crafted a resolution affirming that God always had complete foreknowledge of everything, and 253 members voted in favor. However, it is very interesting that 107 (or one-third) of the ETS members who were present refused to vote for it. Even more interesting is that when the ETS met the next year, according to *Christianity Today*, "More members spoke against the motion than in favor."[1] As a last ditch stand, some classical theists introduced formal motions to expel Clark Pinnock and John Sanders from ETS, but both motions failed to get a majority vote.

## Open Theism Is an Open Question

Why am I telling these stories? It is to surface the fact that our top evangelical theologians are far from reaching a consensus that open theism is an out-and-out heresy. It is simply a different conclusion arrived at by those who take the authority of scripture and the sovereignty of God just as seriously as one another.

To use other terminology, a respectable view is that neither classical theism nor open theism should be categorized as a theological absolute. I like the suggestion that we can classify our theological views as "absolutes" and "interpretations" and "deductions."[2] By this definition, both classical theism and open theism would clearly be deductions. Good, solid, respectable theologians have the freedom to take their choice between the two points of view. Open theism is an open question.

*Christianity Today* magazine clearly agrees that it is an open question. They decided to present both theological points of view to the evangelical community at large by sponsoring a debate in 2001. In fact, they received a grant from the Lily Endowment to cover the expenses. They chose two respected theologians, Christopher Hall to represent classical theism and John Sanders to represent open theism. It spread over two issues. The title was "Does God Know Your Next Move?" In the article they debated 9 questions, but each of them had so much to say that they later put their ideas into a book where they addressed a total of 37 related questions![3]

## Key Questions

In the introduction to the article, Christianity Today raised these questions among others:

- Does God change His mind?
- Does He ever change it in response to our prayers?

- Was God taking a risk in making the human race?[4]

When I began to read what John Sanders said, it reminded me exactly of the frustration that I explained a few pages back. Sanders said, "While in Bible college I read what my theology textbooks said about the nature of God. According to these books, God could not change in any way, could not be affected by us in any respect, and never responded to us. I was shocked!"[5] That is the same thing that kept me and my friends up until 2:00 AM so many nights.

Sanders goes on: "The piety that I had learned from other evangelical Christians was directly opposed to such beliefs. For instance, I was taught that our prayers of petition could influence what God decided to do. Not that God has to do what we ask, but God has decided that some of his decisions will be in response to what we ask or don't ask."[6] This is what I meant when I said that we were concerned that what our professors were teaching us did not always synch very well with reality.

Let me express a personal impression of this debate. John Sanders kept quoting scripture after scripture showing that God has an open mind. Christopher Hall managed to avoid dealing with many of those specific scriptures by citing the wisdom of previous theologians throughout the history of the church who presumably were not swayed from their classical theism by the scriptures that Sanders was quoting.
Key Scriptures

Ever since I began reading Sanders and Pinnock and Boyd, I have kept my eyes open to Bible texts that seem to indicate that God has an open mind. I realize that classical theists have their supply of proof texts as well, but as I said before, I have arrived at a personal conclusion and I am arguing in favor of my conclusion. If I were writing another doctoral dissertation I would take pains to labor both sides, but fortunately this is a practical book on taking dominion, not an academic exercise.

Some of these scriptures are so clear that it is difficult to read them and come to the conclusion that God never changes His mind, that He has decided everything once and for all before the foundation of the world, and that the choices we make do not alter what God has already decided will happen.

Let me point out that some classical theists, not pure Calvinists to be sure, have attempted to compromise by distinguishing between foreknowledge and predestination. The idea behind this is that God did not predetermine certain things because He wanted our choices to count, but that He always knew ahead of time what our choices would be. That idea, however, seems to ignore a key scripture that says, *"For whom He foreknew, He also predestined"* (Rom. 8:29). According to this we shouldn't separate the two. Calvinists try to use this text as proof that God has predestined everything. But notice that it doesn't say outright that God predestines everything. Open theists freely acknowledge that God predestines and thereby has foreknowledge of many things. All they are saying is that God has also chosen to keep an open mind about some other things and, if so, He naturally would not allow Himself to have foreknowledge of that.

Let's take a brief tour through the Bible, highlighting some of the incidents that point toward the conclusion that God has an open mind.

## The Garden of Eden

I dealt with this earlier in the chapter, but, since it is a foundational text for open theism, I think it should be mentioned in this list as well.

## The Flood

Because Adam chose not to obey God, but instead he allowed satan to usurp the authority to take dominion over creation that Adam should have had, the subsequent human race did not develop as God had originally planned. While some individuals were godly, the majority were not. By the time we get to Genesis 6, God was beginning to have second thoughts about humankind.

What was going on? *"Then the Lord saw that the wickedness of man was great in the earth, and that every intent of the thoughts of his heart was only evil continually"* (Gen. 6:5). Obviously, the original plan that God had for humankind was not being fulfilled. God's reaction? *"The Lord was sorry that He had made man on the earth"* (Gen. 6:6).

Let me insert a disclaimer. I am aware that the Hebrew word, *nicham,* translated "sorry" also allows for slightly different nuances and that classical theists naturally gravitate toward those meanings. However, all translations imply some sort of change in God. Please keep in mind that I am not trying to prove that classical theism is *wrong*. I want to affirm that classical theism is one legitimate deduction from biblical data. What I am saying, however, is that open theism is just as legitimate a deduction from the same biblical data. Neither is a theological absolute, as is the deity of Christ. Simply put, my contention is that open theism seems to me to be a much better explanation of biblical data as well as a much more compelling explanation of how God actually works in the world.

What I have just said will apply to most of the Scriptures that I will be citing in this section, so there will be no need to repeat the disclaimer.

The meaning of Genesis 6:5 is a case in point. Let's assume that the Bible was written for average people of normal intelligence. It is not a treatise to be rightly understood only by academic theologians. If so, there is not much question as to how the average reader, unencumbered by theological presuppositions that must be justified in every portion of Scripture, would interpret Genesis 6. It simply says that, while God was the creator of the human race, it turned out so badly at this point in time that He wished He had never done it. The implication is that He was unpleasantly surprised that things had gone this way. If this is the case, it makes no sense to pretend that when God first created human beings, He knew full well that they would get to this point. If that were the case, there would be no surprise, and the fact that He "was sorry" makes no sense.

In fact, God was so sorry that He was ready to terminate the whole human race, as well as all the animals (see Gen. 6:7). Fortunately, He found a man who would obey Him, namely Noah, and humankind was awarded a fresh start after the flood.

## Abraham on Mount Moriah

Most of us know the story of God's testing Abraham by requiring him to sacrifice his son, Isaac. Would Abraham end up obeying God, or wouldn't he? As Genesis 22 tells the story, there was no hesitation on Abraham's part. He took Isaac up on Mount Moriah, built an altar, gathered firewood, took a sharp knife, and was ready to kill him. But of course God intervened and the rest is history.

The question arises as to whether this was a real test that could have gone either way or whether it was all previously scripted by God. For most readers it would be foolish to imagine that this was nothing but a predetermined charade and that God knew ahead of time exactly what Abraham would do. Abraham, like Adam, must have had a true test, and it could have gone either way. How else could it have been a true choice? I believe that God was waiting to see what Abraham would do, and that He was thrilled that Abraham chose to obey Him in this difficult decision. As a result, Abraham gained the favor of God and became one of the great all-time heroes of the faith.

## The Golden Calf

While Moses was up on Mount Sinai receiving the Ten Commandments, Aaron led Israel into idolatry by making the infamous golden calf. God was so upset that He said to Moses, *"I've seen these people, and they are impossible to deal with. Now leave me alone. I'm so angry with them I am going to destroy them. Then I'll make you into a great nation"* (Exod. 32:9-10 GW).

As we know, Moses then interceded on behalf of his people and said, "Don't be so angry. Reconsider your decision to bring this disaster on your people" (Exod. 32:12 GW). The outcome? *"So the Lord reconsidered his threat to destroy his people"* (Exod. 32:14 GW).

It would be difficult to understand this dialogue and the emotions involved if God already knew exactly what He would do ahead of time. It would seem like God was playing games with Moses. But it makes perfect sense if we assume that God had an open mind at this point.

### Hezekiah's Extra Fifteen Years

King Hezekiah was terminally ill. To help him die well, God sent the prophet Isaiah who said, *"Set your house in order, for you shall die, and not live"* (2 Kings 20:1). God's destiny for Hezekiah at that point in time could hardly be stated more simply or more definitively. Hezekiah's time had come.

However, Hezekiah was not a fatalist; he was an activist. He turned to God, he wept, and he prayed fervently. When he did, God said, *"I have heard your prayer, I have seen your tears; surely I will heal you…And I will add to your days fifteen years"* (2 Kings 20:5-6).

This sounds very much like Hezekiah's prayer and his tears were what caused God to change His mind. If God had known ahead of time that Hezekiah would pray so effectively and that He would change his mind, it would not have seemed right for Him to have declared so directly that Hezekiah was going to die as a result of his illness.

## Solomon's Test

When God made Solomon king of Israel, He gave him a very important test. Like the tests of Adam and Abraham, it would only be a valid test if the outcome could have gone either way. If God was only pretending that it could have gone either way because He actually knew ahead of time what Solomon would do, it would not seem like a real test.

God began by offering Solomon a blank check: *"What can I give you?"* (2 Chron. 1:7 GW).

Solomon made the right choice: *"Give me wisdom and knowledge so that I may lead these people"* (2 Chron. 1:10 GW).

The result?

> *God replied to Solomon, "I know this request is from your heart. You didn't ask for riches, fortunes, honor, or the death of those who hate you. You didn't even ask for a long life. Instead, you've asked for wisdom and knowledge to judge my people, over whom I made you king. So wisdom and knowledge will be given to you. I will also give you riches, fortunes, and honor like no other king before or after you* (2 Chronicles 1:11-12 GW).

God obviously was pleased by Solomon's choice.

## Rehoboam's Humility

Rehoboam, king of Judah, was not doing well. The Egyptians, led by King Shishak, were invading his territory, and God was so upset with Rehoboam that he said, *"You have abandoned me, so I will abandon you. I will hand you over to Shishak"* (2 Chron. 12:5 GW). This sounds very much like God had made up His mind.

However, God soon changed His mind. Why? Rehoboam and his leadership team decided to humble themselves. *"'The Lord is right!' they said"* (2 Chron. 12:6 GW).

God liked what they did. *"When the Lord saw that they had humbled themselves, he spoke his word to Shemaiah: 'They have humbled themselves. I will not destroy them.' ...So things went well in Judah"* (2 Chron. 12:7,12 GW). In this case the future was obviously open and Rehoboam's humility shaped the future for the better.

## God Changes His Mind

One of the clearest biblical texts showing that God has an open mind is found in Jeremiah 18. At this point God is talking about Himself and giving us a picture of His true nature. God says:

> At any moment I may decide to pull up a people or a country by the roots and get rid of them. But if they repent of their wicked lives, I will think twice and start over with them. At another time I might decide to plant a people or country, but if they don't cooperate and won't listen to me, I will think again and give

*up on the plans I had for them* (Jeremiah 18:7-10 MSG).

Another way of saying this is that God, on occasions of His choice, can have a Plan A and a Plan B. The way the situation turns out will not depend on something divinely predetermined or foreknown. It will depend, pure and simple, on the choices that people make and God is prepared to shape the future either way.

### Jonah in Nineveh

After Jonah's renowned experience with the whale, he obeyed God and went to Nineveh. He didn't like what he saw. As a prophet of God, he declared God's word as follows: *"In forty days Nineveh will be destroyed"* (Jon. 3:4 GW).

But a very surprising thing happened. *"The people of Nineveh believed God. They decided to fast, and everyone, from the most important to the least important, dressed in sackcloth"* (Jon. 3:5 GW). They said, *"Who knows? God may reconsider his plans and turn from his burning anger so that we won't die"* (Jon. 3:9 GW).

Sure enough, God once again changed His mind. *"God saw what they did, He saw that they turned from their wicked ways. So God reconsidered his threat to destroy them, and he didn't do it"* (Jon. 3:10 GW).

## How Much Does Prayer Matter?

To conclude this chapter, let's get practical. It is one thing to see that the Bible clearly teaches that God has an open mind, but it is another to understand how it applies to our service to God in real life. One of the key areas of Christian life in which open theism is either a spoken or an unspoken assumption is intercessory prayer.

Just bringing this up forces me to think back once again on my seminary days where my professors were classical theists of the Calvinistic type. Since they didn't believe that anything that human beings did could change what God has predestined and foreknew since the foundation of the world, prayer was a bit problematic for them. Why do we pray? What difference will it make if we do pray or if we don't? Does God need us to pray or does He just want us to pray? Their conclusion was that our prayers don't affect God or His plans, but rather they change us. Our prayers help us to fit into whatever God has already planned.

I must admit that for the first thirty years or so of my ministry career, I operated under this passive concept of prayer. In fact, for a period of time I even quit praying, but I'll save that story for another occasion. Why God would have chosen me to help lead the worldwide prayer movement of the 1990s is still a great mystery. However, I am a quick learner, and I soon moved into a more proactive, Spirit-led view of prayer. I was delighted to hear respectable leaders like Walter Wink and Richard Foster and Jack Hayford say things that greatly helped me in my rapid paradigm shift.

## History Belongs to the Intercessors

One of Walter Wink's most-quoted statements is: "History belongs to the intercessors!"[7] That's another way of saying that prayer really makes a difference.

No one has said it better than Richard Foster in his classic, *Celebration of Discipline:* "Certain things will happen in history if we pray rightly."[8]

One of the bolder precursors of open theism is Brother Andrew, who titles his book, *And God Changed His Mind.* He says, "God's plans for us are not chiseled in concrete. Only His character and nature are unchanging. His decisions are not!"[9]

In Jack Hayford's book, *Prayer Is Invading the Impossible,* one of his chapter titles is "If We Don't; He Won't."[10] The idea is not that if we don't pray, God *can't* do something. He is sovereign. I agree with Hayford who says, "We strongly assert the great truth of the sovereignty of God. However, for some today, God's sovereignty has come to mean that God arbitrarily, or randomly, exercises His power, and He somehow has fatefully designed the course of human affairs toward a destiny that involves nothing of human participation."[11] Where does this lead? Hayford responds, "Distorted ideas about God's sovereignty have, as many pastors acknowledge, begotten widespread supposition that to pray boldly is to somehow renounce belief in that truth."[12]

It just so happened that, as I was collecting material for this chapter, I came across a random article by Mary Alice Isleib, one of the most respected and acknowledged intercessors of our day. What she says represents the way that all true intercessors whom I know approach their task. Isleib says, "Every time we pray, if we do so correctly, God's mighty power is released and made available to bring victory and breakthrough into even seemingly impossible situations...In many cities and nations, [God's power] has been withheld for years;

not because of God's reluctance to act, but rather, because God's people have lacked the spiritual understanding necessary to break through and use His power to see their prayers answered."[13]

In order to write this, Mary Alice must have an underlying assumption that God indeed has an open mind.

We can conclude with a Scripture that clearly reveals God's heart as to intercessory prayer, namely Ezekiel 22. God was appalled by the idolatry and other sins of the people of Jerusalem. They had aroused His anger. He said, *"So I sought for a man among them who would make a wall, and stand in the gap before Me on behalf of the land, that I should not destroy it; but I found no one"* (Ezek. 22:30). The job description of intercessors is that they stand in the gap before God. Here it seems clear that if there had been only one intercessor, history could have been different. But since, unfortunately, none was to be found, God said, *"I have consumed them with the fire of My wrath"* (Ezek. 22:31).

Yes, God has an open mind. Yes, prayer makes a difference!

Yes, what we do really matters!

# Chapter 5

# A NEW VITALITY: THE POWER OF THE HOLY SPIRIT

I would not blame anyone who might be puzzled at the title of this chapter. What is so new about the power of the Holy Spirit? Didn't Jesus say to His apostles, *"You shall receive power when the Holy Spirit has come upon you"* (Acts 1:8)? Pentecost occurred almost 2,000 years ago.

Agreed, the power of the Holy Spirit has been available since the birth of the church. However after the first two or three centuries of the church, it became a dormant power, for the most part, until fairly recently. Yes, history has recorded surfacings of the power of the Holy Spirit in the lives and ministries of such as Patrick of Ireland or Boniface or Savanarola and others like them, but none of these affected the warp and woof of the church as a whole.

## The Power Surfaces

It was only around 1900 when the doctrinal affirmation of the power of the Holy Spirit and the historical recognition of the power of the Holy Spirit began to become an operational principle in what is now a critical mass of the church as a whole. The two events that began to turn history some one hundred years ago were the launching of the African Independent Church Movement in Africa and the Pentecostal Movement in America. Because both initially needed to swim upstream against the religious currents of traditional Christianity, it took them a good half a century to begin to exert the widespread influence that they have today.

We can be deeply grateful to researchers like David Barrett and Philip Jenkins for providing us the empirical evidence that the church is now substantially different from what it was fifty years ago. In Chapter 1 we looked at David Barrett's findings that what I am calling the New Apostolic Reformation now constitutes the largest non-Catholic megablock of churches and that it is the fastest growing segment of all. Philip Jenkins' award-winning books, *The New Christendom* and *The New Faces of Christianity*, allow no doubt that God has reshaped the church into a new wineskin for the 21st century.

Notice that the word "new" appears in both of Jenkins' titles. That is the sense in which I am using the word "new" in the title of this chapter on the power of the Holy Spirit. How new is it? We are talking about only the most recent 2.5 percent of Christian history! This is our new wineskin, an essential component in the dynamic of taking back the dominion over creation that Adam lost in the Garden of Eden.

The word "new" is also apropos to my own spiritual pilgrimage. I was ordained into the Christian ministry over 60 years ago. Since then, I managed to spend about half the time uninformed about the operational power of the Holy Spirit and then the other half as an active participant in that power. Because I know both the old wineskin and the new wineskin so well, I feel that I am qualified to at least attempt to encourage some of those who are not yet flowing in the new streams of God to give it a second thought.

## Cessationism

My seminary professors were, by and large, devotees of Benjamin Breckenridge Warfield, the renowned Princeton theologian who strongly argued that the more visible manifestations of the power of the Holy Spirit, such as healings and prophecy and tongues and discernment of spirits and exorcism and miracles, were indeed necessary to help establish the church. That is why we read about them in the New Testament. However, once the canon of Scripture was established and we had the written Word of God they were no longer necessary. Warfield argued that such gifts had "ceased" after the first couple of centuries of the church, and because of that, his view has been called "cessationism."

As I have been observing the rapid growth of Pentecostalism, the Charismatic Movement, the New Apostolic Reformation, and what Philip Jenkins calls The New Christendom, I allowed myself to engage in some wishful thinking. From time to time, I would suggest that cessationism is now on the endangered doctrines list. However, I had some second thoughts when recently the missions agency of one of America's largest denominations passed a ruling that they would accept no new missionaries who practiced speaking in tongues, even as a private prayer language. I was appalled, but it is true. Consequently, I felt that I needed to include this chapter on the power of the Holy Spirit in a book dealing with taking dominion and transforming society. We must not allow ourselves to become spiritually complacent.

The denomination that won't let their missionaries speak in tongues claims that they believe the whole Bible. This seems questionable to me because the Bible plainly teaches that *"These signs will follow those who believe...they will speak with new tongues"* (Mark 16:17).

## "I Will Build My Church!"

Or take, for example, the sequence of events when Jesus and His disciples were in Caesarea Philippi, recorded in Matthew 16. There Jesus asked them who people thought that He was. They said that some thought He was John the Baptist or Elijah or Jeremiah or another of the prophets. That was just setting them up for the real question: *"Who do you say that I am?"* (Matt. 16:15). Peter answered for the whole group and said, *"You are the Christ, the Son of the living God"* (Matt. 16:16). The word "Christ" in the Greek is the same as "Messiah" in Hebrew. After being with Jesus for a year and a half, this was the first time that the disciples were able to verbalize that He was actually the Messiah for whom the Jews had been waiting all this time.

Once they knew for sure who Jesus was, He could then tell them what He had come for. He said, *"On this rock I will build My church"* (Matt. 16:18). That was the first time that Jesus ever used the word "church." Why? Only after they realized that the Messiah had come could He reveal to them that the church had come as well.

Following that, Jesus told them that not only the church, but the kingdom had come. He said, *"I will give you the keys of the kingdom of heaven"* (Matt. 16:19). Now we are getting to the theme of this book, namely taking dominion. Your kingdom come, Your will be done on earth as it is in heaven! Society will be transformed when God's kingdom is activated here and now.

The disciples needed the keys because Jesus had also said that as they were building the church *"the gates of Hades shall not prevail against it"* (Matt. 16:18). The gates of Hades would certainly *try* to stop the growth of the church, but they would not *prevail*. Why not? Because Jesus had given His disciples the keys. The keys would be used to open the gates of Hades so that the gospel of the kingdom could spread. The keys were weapons of spiritual warfare because Jesus said, *"whatever you bind on earth will be bound in heaven, and whatever you loose on earth will be loosed in heaven"* (Matt. 16:19). Binding and loosing will open the gates of Hades. We'll discuss spiritual warfare more in the next chapter.

Meanwhile, I can imagine how excited the disciples would have been. Jesus' talk had been very motivational. They were probably saying words to the effect, "OK, Master! Let's take the world! Lead us on into battle and we will follow!"

# Jesus' Bombshell

But then Jesus dropped the bombshell. He told them that they would be on their own to move into the world and that He would no longer be with them (see Matt. 16:21). Peter didn't like that one bit, and he made the serious mistake of arguing with the Master. That's when Jesus used some of His strongest words, saying to Peter, *"Get behind Me, Satan!"* (Matt. 16:23).

What did this have to do with the power of the Holy Spirit? Jesus let everything calm down for a while before He explained it to them. His explanation is recorded, not in Matthew 16, but in John 16. There Jesus gave them the puzzling news that they would be better off *without* Him than *with* Him. He said, *"I tell you the truth. It is to your advantage that I go away; for if I do not go away, the Helper will not come to you; but if I depart, I will send Him to you"* (John 16:7). Their advantage would be to have the Holy Spirit.

Let me state it theologically. For the purpose of fulfilling the Great Commission, namely discipling the nations or transforming society, the immediate presence of the Third Person of the Trinity is more important than the immediate presence of the Second Person of the Trinity! Jesus is at the right hand of the Father making intercession for us. The operative power of God in our lives and ministries today is the Holy Spirit. That's why it is so unwise to quench the Spirit in any way.

# Endued with Power from on High

To follow up on this, after three years with His disciples and after His death and resurrection, when Jesus was finally ready to go, His instructions were not to go out and start evangelizing the world. Rather He told His disciples to *"tarry in the city of Jerusalem until you are endued with power from on high"* (Luke 24:49). Three years of the best teaching in the world would not suffice. On top of that, they needed the power of the Holy Spirit to effectively preach the message of the kingdom. Fortunately they obeyed, Pentecost came, and the rest is history.

It would be foolish for us to think that anything is different today. Our mandate is to take dominion over God's creation. Social transformation is our goal. No human power is sufficient for such a task. But Jesus' promise is for us: *"You shall receive power when the Holy Spirit has come upon you"* (Acts 1:8).

Think for a moment of changing the social fabric of the city where you are now living. It's an enormous challenge! Yes, we're promised the power of the Holy Spirit, but how much power? That's a very good question, and the answer should be encouraging. Let's begin by thinking of what Jesus once said: *"Most assuredly, I say to you, he who believes in Me, the works that I do he will do also; and greater works than these he will do, because I go to My Father"* (John 14:12). It seems almost unbelievable that any human being could do greater works than Jesus, but none other than Jesus said that it was true. Going to the Father is key because, as we just saw, Jesus said that only when He goes to the Father will He send the Helper, namely the Holy Spirit.

## How Can We Do the Same or Greater Works?

The reason we can expect to do the same or greater works than Jesus today is that we have access to precisely the same power that Jesus used to do all of His works, namely the Holy Spirit. This is so important that it merits a good explanation.

Here is my hypothesis in a nutshell: The Holy Spirit was the source of all of Jesus' power during His earthly ministry. Jesus exercised no power of or by Himself. We can do the same or greater things than Jesus did because we have access to the same power source.

Let's begin thinking this through by reminding ourselves that Jesus has two natures, a divine nature and a human nature. This is one of those theological absolutes that I referred to previously. He isn't half divine and half human. He is 100 percent divine and 100 percent human. The math may not work out, but the theology does. We accept it by faith.

## Why Didn't Jesus Know?

Having asserted that, what, then, is the relationship between the two natures of Jesus? To be more specific, take the problem that Mark 13:32 raises. Jesus was on the Mount of Olives with Peter, James, John, and Andrew. They asked Him when the end would come (see Mark 13:3-4). Jesus gave them a lot of teaching about the last days, then He said, *"But of that day and hour no one knows, not even the angels in heaven, nor the*

*Son, but only the Father"* (Mark 13:32). Jesus admitted that He didn't know when the end was coming. How could this be if He was 100 percent divine? The Father knew, but the Son didn't.

Theologians have paid considerable attention to this perplexing question. Through the years three explanations have been offered, none of which I consider adequate. They are:

## The Total Mystery Theory

The idea here is that we will never know the answer. It is one of those theological mysteries that we cannot fathom. I agree that there are some theological mysteries. One example is how three persons of the Trinity can be of one essence, but I don't agree that the relationship between the two natures of Christ is a mystery.

## The Human Jesus Theory

Some liberal theologians like to teach that Jesus wasn't really God at all and that He was just an exceptional human being. If so, there naturally would be many things that He didn't know. I cannot accept this explanation because I take seriously John 1: *"In the beginning was the Word, and the Word was with God, and the Word was God. ...And the Word became flesh and dwelt among us"* (John 1:1,14). Jesus definitely was God.

## The Two-Channel Theory

This is by far the most common explanation among those who accept the orthodox belief that Jesus was both divine and human. It suggests that during Jesus' earthly ministry, He constantly switched back and forth. Some things He did as God (changing the water into wine, for example) and other things He did as a human (getting hungry and thirsty, for example). This two-channel theory sounds plausible at first, but it doesn't hold up under closer scrutiny.

Mark 13:32 is a case in point. The two-channel theory would say that what Jesus really meant was, *"Humanly speaking,* I don't know when the end will come." Of course, as God He really did know. What is the problem? Very simple. If Jesus was speaking humanly, how did He know that the angels were also ignorant of the date? There is no human way to know how angels think. Would it seem reasonable that Jesus switched channels right in the middle of a sentence? Probably not.

## Taking the Form of a Servant

The best way to understand the relationship of Jesus' human nature to His divine nature is to go to Philippians 2:5-8. It begins by saying that Jesus *"being in the form of God, did not consider it robbery to be equal with God"* (Phil. 2:6). Yes, Jesus was God and He had all the attributes of God. But in the incarnation He became unequal with the Father by receiving a human nature: He *"made Himself of no reputation, taking the form of a bondservant, and coming in the likeness of men"* (Phil. 2:7). Notice that He did not give up His divinity; rather, He became different from the Father and the Holy Spirit by taking on humanity. Attached to this was Jesus' agreement to become obedient to the Father during His incarnation. *"He humbled Himself and became obedient to the point of death, even the death of the cross"* (Phil. 2:8).

Think about Jesus' obedience. It was voluntary. It was temporary. It totally suspended the use (not the possession) of His divine attributes. This means that the only nature Jesus used while on earth was His human nature.

This helps bring meaning to Jesus as the Second Adam. *"The first [Adam] was of the earth, made of dust; the second [Adam] is the Lord from heaven"* (1 Cor. 15:47). Both were created directly by God. Neither was born of the union of human parents. Both were under a covenant of obedience to the Father. Jesus, of course, had access to His divine attributes, but He chose to obey the Father and not use them.

## The Temptations

Satan tempted both of them the same way, aiming to have them break the covenant of obedience to the Father. For Adam it was enticing him to eat the forbidden fruit, and it worked. The First Adam fell. For Jesus it was enticing Him to use His divine attributes by changing stones into bread, by jumping from the temple, and by claiming rightful ownership of the kingdoms of the world. This time satan's ploy did not work, and the Second Adam was victorious.

Reread the gospels in the light of this and you will see that all of Jesus' mighty works, His miracles, His signs and wonders, His prophecies, His deliverance ministry, and the rest can be adequately explained by the supernatural working of the power of the Holy Spirit through Jesus as a human being. For example, He said at one point, *"If I cast out demons by the Spirit of God, surely the kingdom of God has come upon you"* (Matt. 12:28). He didn't cast out demons by His own divine omnipotence, which He could have done. He remained humble and allowed the power of the Holy Spirit to operate through Him.

All of this ended at the cross, as Philippians 2:8 said it would. After His resurrection, Jesus once again had full access to His divine attributes. At that time, His disciples came with a question about when the end would come just like they asked Him in Mark 13:32. But this time Jesus didn't say, "I do not know," because He *did* know. He rather said, "It is not for you to know the times or seasons which the Father has put in His own authority" (Acts 1:7).

## Unlimited Power

This should dissipate any doubts as to how Jesus could tell us, as mere human beings, that we would do the same works that He did and even greater works. The same Holy Spirit who did miracles through Jesus is available to do them through us today. This should give us confidence as we face the challenges of social transformation. There is no human power that can take back the dominion over God's creation that satan usurped. But the Holy Spirit is with us and He offers unlimited power.

Social transformation requires careful planning and strategizing and execution. However, human designs, skillful and fine-tuned as they might be, will not suffice. The kingdom of God will only be established here on earth with full human engagement plus supernatural power. And we would do well not to expect supernatural power to follow what we do humanly but rather to precede what we do and to open the door for implementation.

## Paul in Athens

The apostle Paul learned that lesson well on his second missionary journey. He was fully aware that evangelizing the city of Athens would be a formidable challenge. Athens was the intellectual and philosophical hub of Greco-Roman culture. Paul decided to adjust his mission strategy accordingly. His usual procedure was to start with the local synagogue community, which he did (see Acts 17:17). Then, for whatever reason, he began listening to some philosophers who persuaded him to come onto their turf, namely the Areopagus. Paul, a learned intellectual in his own right, did some research and came up with information on things like the unknown god. The philosophers liked to argue, so Paul set out to argue them into believing the truth of God.

I know that many homiletics professors claim that Paul's sermon on Mars Hill was his best one. Intellectually it may well have been. But evangelistically it was anything but. There in the Athens Areopagus, Paul experienced the worst nightmare of a public speaker. His audience became so unruly they didn't even allow him the courtesy of finishing his address. They laughed him to scorn. They interrupted him and said words to the effect, "Thanks, but no thanks!" Paul ended up with a few converts, but we later hear nothing of a solid church in Athens. It was Paul's most unfruitful evangelistic attempt.

What did Paul learn from his painful experience in Athens? He learned that no human efforts, brilliant as they might be, can upstage the sheer power of the Holy Spirit. In one of his most transparent moments, Paul opens his heart about Athens to the believers who came to Christ on his next stop, namely Corinth.

When Paul writes 1 Corinthians, he says, *"I, brethren, when I came to you, did not come with excellence of speech or of wisdom [as I just did in Athens!]…and my speech and my preaching were not with persuasive words of human wisdom [like they were in Athens!], but in the demonstration of the Spirit and of power"* (1 Cor. 2:1,4). The lesson for us is *"that [our] faith should not be in the wisdom of men but in the power of God…for the kingdom of God is not in word but in power"* (1 Cor. 2:5; 4:20).

## Taking Dominion

This relates directly to taking dominion. For hundreds and hundreds of years, sad to say, it would not have been possible for the Holy Spirit to speak to the churches about social transformation as He is doing today. The reason is that the church was not tapping into the supernatural power that has always been available. I often wonder about John Calvin. As we saw in Chapter 2, Calvin accurately understood the cultural mandate. He taught that God's people have a responsibility to bring society into alignment with the kingdom of God. But his blind spot was his lack of touch with the power of the Holy Spirit. While I mentioned Benjamin Breckenridge Warfield as a recent theological advocate of cessationism, it should be added that Warfield's chief source was

John Calvin.[1] History could have turned out quite differently in Europe had Calvin understood how essential supernatural power is for implementing the cultural mandate and transforming society.

Even among some leaders today who should know better, the power of the Holy Spirit is not front and center. I agree with Robin McMillan who says, "To transform society, each generation must operate at a higher spiritual level than the preceding one by having a progressive experience of His power. Sadly, some Christians have had very little experience with the supernatural dimension of God. Many other believers have known His power, but allowed their experience to diminish over time."[2]

## The Danger of Routinization

McMillan is putting his finger on a danger that we must be acutely aware of. As sociologists of religion from Max Weber to Margaret Poloma have been pointing out, there is a built-in tendency for new, high-vitality religious movements to routinize. Numerous observers, both insiders and outsiders, have pointed out that this has been happening in the Pentecostal movement in general. Many second generation Pentecostal leaders, embarrassed by their parents' exuberance and by the label "Holy Rollers," have determined to make their churches more respectable. Surveys have shown, for example, that a large percentage of members of U.S. Pentecostal churches do not speak in tongues.

I clearly recall being present in an adult Sunday School class where one of the members was reporting on her recent two-week vacation. On one of her Sundays away she had worshiped in a Pentecostal Church in Canada and on the other she had worshiped in a Presbyterian Church in California. With a considerable degree of satisfaction in her voice, she said, "And you really couldn't tell much difference between the two churches!" I politely kept my silence, but I was appalled. A generation ago the two churches would have been as different as a rock concert and a Beethoven symphony. But what had happened? The Presbyterian Church had stayed true to form. But the Pentecostal church had succeeded in becoming "respectable." Part and parcel of this is the tendency to dilute and diminish their activation of supernatural power.

Here is what sociologist Margaret Poloma has found:

> Despite the evidence of ongoing religious experiences, few observers would question that the charismatic fervor of the early Pentecostals had been domesticated over the decades. Although charisma is still very much a part of [their religious lifestyle—ed.], in theory as well as in practice, there has been a noteworthy shift from an emphasis on "magical charisma" supported by prophetic leaders to priestly or more routinized forms.[3]

## Let's Move On with Power!

This danger of routinization, with its accompanying reduction of the applied power of the Holy Spirit, is equally present in the Charismatic Movement, the offspring of the Pentecostal Movement, and the New Apostolic Reformation, the offspring of the Charismatic Movement. If we are not aware of this possibility and consequently on our guard, we could soon find ourselves reversing what we saw concerning the apostle Paul and end up moving from Corinth back to Athens. Instead of the power of God, we could become satisfied with enticing words of man's wisdom. I don't anticipate that such a thing will happen, but if it does our efforts to take dominion and experience the presence of God's kingdom in our societies will predictably be of little avail.

Churches of the Second Apostolic Age must continue to be churches distinguished by supernatural power. If Bill Hamon's book *The Day of the Saints* is correct in its prophetic outlook, supernatural power will not be routinized in the apostolic churches, but rather it will increase greatly, diffused throughout the churches. Signs and wonders will no longer be the domain of superstars or healing evangelists, but they will become part and parcel of the normal experience of all the saints. Such a thing is already commonplace throughout Philip Jenkins' "global South."

The last time I was in Nigeria, for example, I was talking to an ordinary evangelist, whose name I don't even remember. I asked if signs and wonders were part of his normal ministry, and he assured me that they were. I then asked, "Have you ever seen the dead raised?" He answered, "Oh, yes, of course." I then asked, "How many have you personally seen raised from the dead?" He paused for a moment, shook his head, and replied, "I don't really know. I can't remember!" I was stunned! Then I thought of Jesus sending out His disciples. He routinely told them to preach the kingdom of God, *"heal the sick, cleanse the lepers, raise the dead, cast out demons*" (Matt. 10:7-8). Why should I have expected anything less in Nigeria?

And the bigger question, of course, is why should we expect anything less here in America? We obviously shouldn't. Let's tune in to the supernatural power of the Holy Spirit as we obey God and move into whatever is necessary for "Your kingdom to come, Your will to be done on earth as it is in heaven!"

Chapter 6

# A NEW REALITY: THIS MEANS WAR!

We have seen that the Second Adam, Jesus Christ, came to seek and to save that which was lost, meaning the First Adam's loss of the dominion over creation that God had designed for him and for the human race. Jesus came to *"destroy the works of the devil"* (1 John 3:8). Satan might have usurped Adam's authority over creation in the Garden of Eden, but Jesus came with the aggressive intention of turning history back around.

## A Full-Scale Invasion

What were the works of the devil that Jesus came to destroy? They were obviously the misery and the systemic poverty and the injustice and the oppression that satan had succeeded in inflicting on the human race since the Garden of Eden. Satan's titles *"prince of the power of the air"* (Eph. 2:2) or *"ruler of this world"* (John 14:30) imply that he has a kingdom. He rules a belligerent hierarchy of evil. On a global scale, this kingdom of darkness had not been directly challenged before the coming of the Second Adam. But when Jesus did come, He was launching a full-scale invasion.

It is reminiscent of the European Theater of World War II. The Allies, led by Britain and America, were determined to turn Adolph Hitler's years of evil aggression around. Hitler had conquered Europe and he was attempting to bombard Great Britain into submission. The Allies decided to go on the offensive and to stage a massive invasion of Europe on the beaches of Normandy, France. D-Day was a risky and costly military operation, but the Allies succeeded in securing their beachhead. Once they did, everyone knew that the war in Europe was over and that Hitler had been defeated.

But in reality the war wasn't over. Some of the most ferocious battles still had to be fought before Hitler was finally brought to his knees. However, the courage and dedication of the Allies prevailed and extracted an unconditional surrender from Germany.

## The War Is Not Yet Over!

Jesus' coming in the flesh, dying on the cross, and being raised from the dead was the equivalent of satan's D-Day. Once Jesus brought the kingdom of God to earth, a spiritual beachhead had been secured. The ultimate war was won and satan had been defeated on the cross just like Hitler had been defeated on the beaches of Normandy. However, the spiritual war is not yet over by far. For 2,000 years the kingdom of God has been advancing with force, and God's plan is for it to continue with increasing vigor until Jesus decides to return.

Whether satan knows he is defeated or not is unclear. In any case, he certainly does not intend to go quietly. For the church, this means war!

One of Jesus' better-known titles is "Prince of Peace." However, look what Jesus also said: *"Do not think that I came to bring peace on earth. I did not come to bring peace but a sword"* (Matt. 10:34). How can these two seemingly contradictory facts be reconciled?

In the real world, more often than not, the only way to attain peace is to win a war. My generation, for example, has lived mostly in peace. Why? Because we won World War II. I was 15 when it ended. In comparison, the Korean War and the Vietnam War and the Cold War were nothing but flashes in the pan. Even throughout the history of Israel in the Old Testament, the times of peace almost always followed victory in war. For example, Solomon had peace only because his father, David, had been willing to wage war.

## Saul's Failure

The case of Saul shows how seriously God takes war. Saul was obviously a king of God's own choice. God had planned an incredible destiny for him. One of his first assignments from God was to *"go and attack Amalek, and utterly destroy all that they have, and do not spare them. But kill both man and woman, infant and nursing child, ox and sheep, camel and donkey"* (1 Sam. 15:3). Saul went to war, but what did he choose to do? *"Saul…spared Agag [king of the Amalekites] and the best of the sheep, the oxen, the fatlings, the lambs, and all that was good, and [was] unwilling to utterly destroy them"* (1 Sam. 15:9). Saul did not misunderstand what God had commanded; he simply chose not to obey.

God was deeply disappointed. This was one of the incidents where, as I explained in Chapter 4, He had apparently chosen to keep an open mind. It was not God who predestined and foreknew that Saul would disobey Him. It was Saul's free choice. When He saw what Saul did, God said, *"I greatly regret that I have set up Saul as king"* (1 Sam. 15:11). He originally thought that Saul would make the right choices and He was very sorry when Saul let Him down. So God changed His mind about Saul and went to a Plan B. Saul even tried to repent, but it was too late. In the very next chapter, David is anointed as Saul's successor!

Fortunately, we are now living under a new covenant, not the old covenant when God was directing His people to wage physical war and to destroy their enemies. With the new covenant, Jesus brought the kingdom of God. Our battles are no longer physical; they are spiritual. Jesus said, *"From the days of John the Baptist until now the kingdom of heaven suffers violence, and the violent take it by force"* (Matt. 11:12). We will not take dominion by remaining passive. We will only take dominion if the body of Christ becomes violent and declares war on the enemy!

## From Heaven to Earth

The cosmic overview of this war is found in Revelation 12. Let's look at it carefully:

- There is a war. *"And war broke out in heaven: Michael and his angels fought [against] the dragon; and the dragon and his angels fought"* (Rev. 12:7).

Satan obviously has a powerful army of evil under his command. The war starts in heaven.

- The final victory is settled. *"[The dragon and his angels] did not prevail, nor was a place found for them in heaven any longer"* (Rev. 12:8).

- Satan is cast down. *"The great dragon was cast out, that serpent of old, called the Devil and Satan, who deceives the whole world"* (Rev. 12:9).

- Satan takes the war from heaven to earth. *"He was cast to the earth, and his angels were cast out with him"* (Rev. 12:9). The battles now must be fought by those of us here on earth.

- Satan is more ferocious now than he has ever been. *"For the devil has come down to you, having great wrath, because he knows that he has a short time"* (Rev. 12:12). It would stand to reason that as time moves on the enemy will become more desperate and even more dangerous.

- Satan wars against God's people. *"And the dragon was enraged with the woman, and he went to make war with the rest of her offspring, who keep the commandments of God and have the testimony of Jesus Christ"* (Rev. 12:17). If you and I have the testimony of Jesus Christ, satan is warring against us. We may not like war. We may even choose to be in denial. But it makes no difference—we are definitely in war, like it or not.

- God wins! Three things ultimately win the war: (1) What Jesus has done: *"they overcame him by the blood of the Lamb,"* (2) What we say: "by the word of their testimony," and (3) What we do about it: *"they did not love their lives to the death"* (Rev. 12:11). We must not be passive. We must be fully committed to destroying the works of the devil even if it might mean our lives. Every Allied soldier storming the beaches of Normandy on D-Day was committed to giving his life if necessary. Why should we be any less committed to extending the kingdom of God?

Not only is the church expected to war, but it is expected to win the war!

## Broadening the Agenda

Spiritual warfare will undoubtedly increase both in intensity and in effectiveness now that we are in the Second Apostolic Age. It is a curious fact that the church in general seemed to be content with a minimal engagement in spiritual warfare previous to the 1990s. For example, when I took my theological training in the 1950s and 1960s, spiritual warfare wasn't on any of my professors' radar screens to my recollection.

During my participation in the leadership of the Lausanne Committee for World Evangelization (LCWE) in the 1970s and 1980s, spiritual warfare was not on our agenda. Remarkably, we were intent on strategizing how to win the world to Christ almost as if the devil had gone into hibernation somewhere. Even the Pentecostals in our midst, who probably should have known better, did not attempt to direct our attention to overcoming the malignant principalities and powers intent on seeing that satan would maintain his dominion over creation as long as he possibly could.

A dramatic change, attributable, at least in my view, only to the sovereign move of the hand of God, began during the International Congress on World Evangelization held in Manila in 1989. Although it was unplanned by the program committee, no fewer than five of the speakers in Manila chose to address the topic of what we were calling "territorial spirits." I happened to be one of the five. While there, I sensed very clearly that God was assigning me to help take ongoing leadership in this area.

## Strategic-Level Spiritual Warfare

I soon began to convene a series of high-level consultations, bringing together a couple of dozen leaders who had shown interest in what came to be called "strategic-level spiritual warfare." We named it the Spiritual Warfare Network (SWN). I compiled a book of the writings of 19 authors who, I discovered, had at least addressed the subject at one point in time. It was published in the U.S. as Engaging the Enemy and in England as Territorial Spirits. Now it has been reissued by Destiny Image with the title Territorial Spirits.

While doing this I was teaching at Fuller Theological Seminary. Inevitably the media, both secular and Christian, became interested in this highly innovative and quite controversial development, and the media attention succeeded in pulling a number of seminary theologians out of their comfort zones. One thing led to another, and I was summoned before the Faculty Senate to defend myself in what, to all intents and purposes, amounted to a heresy trial. Fortunately I had previously been awarded academic tenure and no one was able to prove that what I was teaching had violated any part of the seminary's statement of faith. That made my job secure, but it did not immediately quench the criticism.

Eventually things calmed down and the upshot was that spiritual warfare began to be taken very seriously by significant segments of the body of Christ. The literature on the subject began to mushroom in the 1990s and the 2000s. Even many of the theologians and scholars have become curious as to whether demons and evil spirits and principalities and powers really do exist today, especially after reading Philip Jenkins' *The New Faces of Christianity*. Jenkins, a highly regarded Penn State scholar, highlights the new massive and exploding church in the "global South," pointing out the differences between it and the rather routine and aging Northern church as we know it. Jenkins says, for example, "Overwhelmingly, global South churches teach a firm belief in the existence of evil and in the reality of the devil."[1] He then quotes Olusegun Obsanjo, currently president of Nigeria, as saying, "Doubting the existence of the devil or Satan is like doubting the existence of sin. Noticing the influence and the effect of

occultism, esotericism, and secure cults in our society and particularly in our institutions of higher learning, we can hardly
deny the existence of demonic or devilish beings."[2]

Absorbing such things is not easy for traditional Northern
theologians. Jenkins goes on to comment, "Most Northern
readers today would label believers in demons and witchcraft
irredeemably premodern, prescientific, and probably preliter-
ate; and such beliefs would cast doubt on believers' claims to
an authentic or intelligent religion."[3] No wonder I was called
in to address the Faculty Senate!

## Apostles Are Warriors

The timing of this new direction for the body of Christ was
remarkably parallel to the emergence of the biblical government of the church which we saw in Chapter 1. It was only in
the 1990s that the gift and office of apostle began to be recognized and accepted. Previously the church had been led largely
by pastor-teachers and administrators. The responsibility of
pastors is to care for, nurture, and comfort the flock. Very few
pastors have either the gifts or the temperament to mobilize
an army for war. Apostles, on the other hand, do. For the most
part apostles are warriors. They take pains to get to know the
enemy, to develop skill in the employment of the weapons of
spiritual warfare, and to motivate those who are called to the
front lines.

With this in mind, it is quite understandable that the Holy
Spirit would not begin speaking to the churches about high-
level attacks against satan and his forces of evil until apostles
were on the scene. Now that they are, there is no turning back.

The kingdom of God will expand throughout the earth. Satan is ferocious because he knows that his end is getting nearer and nearer. His final demise, like Hitler's, is just a matter of time.

## We Must Overcome

Meanwhile, we as the body of Christ must overcome. We must take back what the enemy has stolen. Jesus Himself wrote seven letters to churches, which we find in chapters 2 and 3 of Revelation. It is remarkable that in every one of the seven He told the people in those churches that they should "overcome." And each time He attached a wonderful promise for those who were willing to go to war and overcome the enemy. Here is the list:

- Ephesus (Rev. 2:7): You'll eat from the tree of life.

- Smyrna (Rev. 2:11): You'll escape the second death.

- Pergamos (Rev. 2:17): You'll get some hidden manna.

- Thyatira (Rev. 2:26): You'll have power over nations.

- Sardis (Rev. 3:5): Your name will be in the book of life.

- Philadelphia (Rev. 3:12): You'll be a pillar in God's temple.

- Laodicea (Rev. 3:21): You'll sit with Jesus on
  His throne!

What, exactly, does "overcome" mean? The Greek word for overcome is *nikao*. This is easy to remember because it is the root of the boy's name "Nicholas" or the girl's name "Nicole." That's what some parents name their child whom they hope will be a winner. It is also the root of Nike shoes, backing the creative commercial idea that if you wear Nikes you'll be sure to win the game!

## Overcoming Is Spiritual Warfare

What is nikao intended to mean in the Bible? Here is what the International Dictionary of New Testament Theology says: "In the New Testament *nikao* almost always presupposes the conflict between God and opposing demonic powers."[4] In other words, *nikao* is a biblical word for spiritual warfare, mentioned seven times by Jesus in Revelation 2 and 3.

We only know of Jesus' using the word *nikao* two other times. One is the famous passage where Jesus says, *"I have overcome (nikao) the world"* (John 16:33). The other is in Luke 11:22: *"When a stronger than he comes upon him and overcomes (nikao) him."*

Let me explain the second one. The Pharisees were following Jesus around trying to find something they could accuse Him of doing. They watched him cast a demon out of a mute man so that the mute man spoke for the first time in his life. As they were trying to explain how such a thing could happen, one of the Pharisees suggested that Jesus must have been using the power of Beelzebub, a well-known demonic principality. So Jesus responded to what they said about Beelzebub:

- *"If I cast out demons with the finger of God, surely the kingdom of God has come upon you"* (Luke 11:20). The "finger of God" means the Holy Spirit (see Matt. 12:28).

- *"When a strong man, fully armed, guards his own palace, his goods are in peace"* (Luke 11:21). The strong man obviously is a demonic principality. The strong man has armament and is prepared to war. He protects his goods, which means the illegal dominion he has over society especially over unsaved souls. Obviously, if nothing happens to his armor, he maintains dominion.

- *"But when a stronger than he comes upon him"* (Luke 11:22). The stronger one is the Holy Spirit, the power by which Jesus said He cast out demons in verse 20. Remarkably, this is the same Holy Spirit who is in us! Jesus said, *"You shall receive power when the Holy Spirit has come upon you"* (Acts 1:8). With the power of the Holy Spirit we can confidently confront the strong man.

- *"But when a stronger than he comes upon him and overcomes him"* (Luke 11:22). "Overcomes" is nikao, the second time Jesus uses the word outside of Revelation.

Let's not miss the importance of this for taking dominion. Taking dominion is not just praying and passively expecting God to do it for us. That is not God's design. Taking dominion is actively confronting the strong men or the principalities and powers under satan's command and overcoming them with the power of the Holy Spirit in us. When we do that we take from him all his armor in which he trusted and we divide his spoils (see Luke 11:22). God's people assume their rightful dominion over creation. We are overcomers!

## The Theaters of the War

All spiritual warfare is not the same. When the Spiritual Warfare Network (SWN) began its series of meetings in the early 1990s, a top agenda item was to label and define what the significantly different areas of spiritual warfare actually were. The SWN concluded that it would be helpful to distinguish three theaters of our warfare:

- Ground-level spiritual warfare: This is casting demons out of individuals, most commonly known as deliverance ministry.

- Occult-level spiritual warfare: This is not confronting individual demons, but rather dealing with more organized activities of evil spirits such as would be found in witchcraft, voodoo, Eastern religions, Satanism, Freemasonry, Santería, New Age, Macumba, magic, Wicca, and the like.

- Strategic-level spiritual warfare: This enters the invisible realm of principalities and powers of darkness, which often take the form of territorial spirits assigned to keep whole geographical areas, social spheres, or cultural groups in bondage to evil. This is clearly the most demanding area of spiritual warfare. It can result in casualties if not done wisely, according to spiritual protocol, and under the specific direction and assignment of the Holy Spirit. Having said this, much of the warfare directly related to taking dominion and social transformation will obviously be on the strategic level. For that reason, the focus of this chapter is on strategic-level spiritual warfare.

## Warfare in Ephesus

To elaborate a bit, consider Paul's ministry in Ephesus. Ephesus stands out as Paul's most successful evangelistic effort. For example, *"[In two years] all who dwelt in Asia [the province in which Ephesus was located] heard the word of the Lord Jesus, both Jews and Greeks"* (Acts 19:10). Not surprisingly, Paul engaged in spiritual warfare on all three levels while evangelizing Ephesus. Let's look at them:

- Ground-level spiritual warfare: *"Now God worked unusual miracles by the hands of Paul, so that even handkerchiefs or aprons were brought from his body to the sick, and the diseases left them and the evil spirits went out of them"* (Acts 19:11-12). Casting out demons was part of the normal routine of evangelization as Jesus, on many occasions, said it should be.

- Occult-level spiritual warfare: Ephesus was the vortex of magic in the Roman Empire. It had the most renowned schools of magic where the most skillful magicians taught and practiced. Per capita, there were probably more magicians in Ephesus than anywhere else. Paul not only engaged the magicians, but he ministered very powerfully to them. *"Many of those who had practiced magic brought their books together and burned them in the sight of all. And they counted up the value of them, and it totaled fifty thousand pieces of silver"* (Acts 19:19). The value in today's economy would be around $4 million. There must have been quite a few converted magicians to feed a fire like that!

- Strategic-level spiritual warfare: The territorial spirit over Ephesus was the notorious Diana of the Ephesians. Her temple was one of the seven wonders of the ancient world. More than that, it was said to be the first historical equivalent to the World Bank. While Paul didn't engage her one on one, her dominion had been weakened to the extent that her idols were losing their power, the silversmiths who crafted them were going out of business, and they staged a riot on behalf of Diana and against Paul. In their minds, there was a cause-and-effect relationship between Diana's embarrassing occult impotence and Paul's presence in Ephesus (see Acts 19:23-41).

Although we don't find it in the Bible, subsequent history indicates that the apostle John assumed leadership of the church in Ephesus some years after Paul left. The eminent Yale historian, Ramsay MacMullen, tells us that John, unlike Paul, did take on Diana directly. John went into her temple and engaged in strategic-level spiritual warfare. According to MacMullen, in the temple John prayed, "O God…at whose name every idol takes flight and every demon and every unclean power: now let the demon that is here take flight in thy name!"[5] When he spoke that word through the power of the Holy Spirit, the sacred altar of Diana split into pieces and half the temple fell down! From that point on Ephesus became the center of world Christianity for the next 200 years. This is one of the best examples of how spiritual warfare can assist in taking dominion.

## The Total Picture

Let's pause to recall the graphic from the Introduction that places the operational components of social transformation into the total picture. Note that dealing with issues of the land provides the foundation for the whole process and overarching everything is the need to confront cosmic powers in such a way that the entire atmosphere is open to connect heaven to earth. Paul has this in mind when he urges that *The manifold wisdom of God might be made known by the church to the principalities and powers in the heavenly places"* (Eph. 3:10). For the church, once again, this means war!

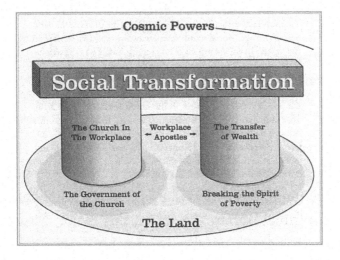

Notice how "The Land" forms the arena on which social transformation will occur. The Bible says, *"If My people who are called by My name will humble themselves, and pray and seek My face, and turn from their wicked ways, then I will hear from heaven, and will forgive their sin and heal their land"* (2 Chron. 7:14). Land can be polluted. Bloodshed, tyranny, oppression, trauma, injustice, broken covenants, sexual perversion, corruption, idolatry, and war can provide entry points for principalities and powers to take dominion. When they do, the land comes under spiritual bondage and it needs healing.

## Usinsk, Russia

The Russian town of Usinsk actually saw this happen. It had experienced an oil boom, then an oil bust. Pastor Schenjazara-penko, who understood the principles behind healing the land, took leadership. He described Usinsk like this: "General poverty, unemployment, crime, drugs, unfinished buildings and the growth of heathen cults were the town's major characteristics."[6] In fact the mayor had announced publicly that all those who could possibly leave should do so.

What were the "principles behind healing the land" that Schenjazarapenko applied to Usinsk?

## Prayer

As I have been saying in this chapter, spiritual warfare is necessary to open heaven and push back the devil's evil forces of destruction in our societies. Prayer is the absolute foundation for spiritual warfare. However, this is not just any kind of prayer. It is not pastoral prayer in this case; it is apostolic prayer. It is not pious, religious prayer; it is prophetic prayer. It is not defensive prayer; it is offensive prayer. In Usinsk's case, it took only a small group of believers who knew how to pray this way and who prayed aggressively and powerfully for four months.

## Spiritual Mapping

Strategic, prophetic prayer is only fully effective if it is properly targeted. As George Otis, Jr. would say, we need to base our spiritual warfare on "informed intercession."[7] In my book *Breaking Strongholds in Your City*, Otis has a chapter along with other experts, and at the end you will find 60 questions that you need to ask and answer to be able to target your prayers for social transformation. Schenjazarapenko and his group did their spiritual mapping of Usinsk so that their prayers were focused on the major strongholds that the territorial spirits had established.

## Identificational Repentance

Sins, particularly social sins, of the past can be identified, dealt with spiritually by those who are living today and who may not have actually committed those sins, and remitted. That is part of the humbling of ourselves, praying, and turning from wicked ways that we find in 2 Chronicles 7:14. Schenjazarapenko says, "We repented of the sins of the past (civil war, gulags, rebellions) and the present, including the satanic rituals in cemeteries and to so-called 'altars of death' where abortions were performed."[8] Since such sins of past and present pollute the land, they must be remitted if the land is to be properly cleansed.

## Prayer Walking and Prophetic Acts

While, of course, we pray a good bit in church, warfare prayer takes us outside the church into the community. Prayer within the church is mostly pastoral, but outside the church it becomes more apostolic and prophetic. It is true that prayer knows no boundaries, but it is also true that on-site prayer has proven to be more effective in dislodging principalities and powers of darkness than distance prayers. The intercessors in Usinsk "walked around the town for months, performed every conceivable symbolic act [these are also known as "prophetic acts"—ed.], including praying on Nawarna-Rodne, a mountain nearby with statues of Lenin and the so-called 'Queen of Heaven.'"[9]

## Reconciliation

The Bible says that God has given us the ministry of rec-onciliation (see 2 Cor. 5:18). This is a spiritual principle, but it plays out on the natural level. Almost every social group can pinpoint other groups whom they have wounded or who have wounded them at one time or another. This often involves war or racism or discrimination or unfair trade or border dis-putes or oppression and things like that. The resulting hatred and prejudice and bitterness and anger can create areas where demonic spirits can lodge and produce social tensions that lead to poverty and misery. However, such social malaise can be healed through Holy Spirit-led reconciliation. The believ-ers in Usinsk held public reconciliation services with Chris-tians from Germany, Switzerland, and other nations to heal past wounds.

# Life Returns to Usinsk

Here is an example of measurable social transformation. Schenjazarapenko reports: "A new spirit came into the town. Unfinished buildings were completed, houses repainted, drugs have almost completely vanished, and the police and mafia are equally confused. Wages have risen, children's playgrounds have been cleaned up, the birth rate is again higher than the death rate, and crime has sunk by 60%. There is no more unemployment—quite the opposite: people from the region travel to work here."[10] The people of Usinsk, both believers and unbelievers, are saying, "Life has returned!" The life they are referring to is, of course, the kingdom of God coming here on earth as it is in heaven. God's people are taking dominion in Usinsk. They are healing the land.

## From Petition to Proclamation

When the Russian believers went to the mountain that had statues of Lenin and the Queen of Heaven, they engaged in strategic-level spiritual warfare. Most likely on that mountain they did what most experienced strategic-level intercessors would do, namely switching from petition to proclamation.

Both forms of intercession are biblical. Both, for example, are found in Job 22:27-28:

- Petition: *"You will make your prayer to Him, He will hear you"* (Job 22:27).

- Proclamation: *"You will also declare a thing, and it will be established for you"* (Job 22:28).

In proclamation, we are not asking God to do something. We are declaring, with the authority of God, that such-and-such a thing that we know to be the will of God will happen. It is like when Moses was on the banks of the Red Sea and God said to him, *"Why do you cry to Me? ...Lift up your rod, and stretch out your hand over the sea and divide it"* (Exod. 14:15-16). God told Moses to stop his petitioning and to move to proclamation. Here is how Richard Foster describes proclamation: "We are calling forth the will of the Father upon the earth. Here we are not so much speaking *to* God as speaking *for* God. We are not asking God to do something; rather we are using the authority of God to command something done."[11]

It goes without saying that in order to proclaim into being the will of God it is obviously necessary first to hear from God. Prayer is not only one way as many suppose; it is two way. We speak to God and He also speaks to us. Proclamation is only effective if we are proclaiming the will of God for that particular situation. I recall, for example, that I was in a public meeting in Germany during the mad cow disease epidemic when God told me to make an apostolic declaration against the disease. I did this in front of 2,500 people, and that turned out to be the last day a case of mad cow disease was reported. I didn't ask God to stop the epidemic; rather, I commanded it to stop by the authority I had through the blood of Jesus Christ. It did!

As a matter of curiosity, I checked out five cases of raising the dead in the New Testament because that is such a relatively high-profile miracle. One incident involved Peter, one Paul, and three Jesus. In every one of them proclamation (such as *"Lazarus come forth!"*) was used. This may indicate that the higher the level of prayer, the more proclamation rather than petition is called for.

## Standing Rock

Here in America, the ones who are, by and large, the most familiar with issues of the land and accompanying strategic-level warfare are Native Americans. My friend Apostle Jay Swallow was directly involved in a notable example of this. On the Standing Rock Sioux Reservation an epidemic of suicides suddenly started in 1997. Pastors of all denominations started praying against it, but the suicides only increased. At one point there were over 60 suicides in two months. The leaders decided to call in Jay, who is a Southern Cheyenne, and who has built a reputation for taking authority over the land.

When Swallow arrived at Standing Rock, he first convened 120 of the top Sioux leaders including the tribal chiefs, witch doctors, of the traditional pagan religion, teachers, social workers, and government agents. Jay set up the ground rules. He told them that he had the authority to break the curse of suicide on the reservation, but in order for him to proceed he needed their full backing in whatever he decided to do. This unusual request from a Christian apostle who was a stranger to most of them required two days of intense discussion and interaction. However, the leaders were so desperate by then that they decided to give Jay the blank check he requested.

The petition-type pastoral intercession that had been prayed for months by the denominational leaders undoubtedly did much to open the way for Jay Swallow to come to Standing Rock and also to prepare the hearts of the 120 leaders to receive his ministry there. However, for the actual confrontation with the demonic forces in the invisible world, which were causing the misery, proclamation, not petition, was called for. On December 27, 2001, Jay Swallow issued an authoritative apostolic decree that suicides would cease on Standing Rock. From that day on, for over three years, not a single suicide *attempt* was recorded on the reservation. Since then, although a suicide did occur, the epidemic has not returned!

If we are serious about taking back the dominion that the devil has stolen, we must be just as serious about the spiritual warfare necessary to displace him.

# Chapter 7

# A NEW SCENARIO: THE CHURCH IN THE WORKPLACE

At this point, it is time that we paused a moment to connect with the overall purpose and thrust of this book. It is a book on the kingdom of God. It is a book on social transformation. It is a book on taking dominion. I chose to use Dominion! as the title because it radiates the idea of action. God wants His kingdom to come, He wants to see our societies transformed, but He has determined to use us, His people here on earth, to partner with Him in order to make it happen. I included a chapter on the openness of God so that we all could realize biblically how important our action, namely what we choose to do, really is in God's strategic design for the future of humankind.

The social transformation graphic that I have been using throughout the book is intended to highlight the most crucial pieces in the divine equation for social transformation. And it shows how they fit together as well:

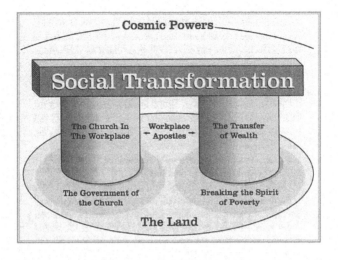

Notice that the only part of the schematic that has arrows indicating action is also the only part referring to certain individuals, namely workplace apostles. The reason for this is that, in my best analysis of the social transformation dynamic, the role of workplace apostles is absolutely essential. I do not believe that we will see the social transformation we desire unless our workplace apostles are properly activated.

## Workplace Apostles?

I realize that for some the notion that there even are such things as "workplace apostles" is a new thought. This is to be expected whenever there is a shifting into a new season of God. Social scientists, as I have mentioned, help us by distinguishing between early adopters, middle adopters, and late adopters when any significant new innovation is introduced to the public. As far as the urgency of taking dominion is concerned, the body of Christ is probably finishing the early adopter phase and beginning to move into the middle adopter phase.

My desire in this chapter is to help as many of us as possible understand workplace apostles and to be aware of the crucial task that they have in this hour. The left-hand pillar above shows where workplace apostles come from, namely the church in the workplace. And the foundation underlying this component is the biblical government of the church. Just as a reminder, I used the first chapter to attempt to lay the foundation of the biblical government of the church. In it I had a good bit to say about the gift and office of apostle in the church in general. We are now in the Second Apostolic Age. Yes, apostles are with us. But apostles are not all the same. Let me explain.

First Corinthians 12 is the most detailed chapter in the Bible on spiritual gifts. Among the many gifts listed appears the gift of apostle (see 1 Cor. 12:28, 29). The chapter begins by saying, *"There are diversities of gifts, but the same Spirit. There are differences of ministries, but the same Lord. And there are diversities of activities, but it is the same God who works all in all"* (1 Cor. 12:4-6). What does this show us? Every apostle would obviously have the gift of apostle, but not all apostles would have the same ministry or activity. This means that apostles in the workplace would be expected to have different ministries and activities than those apostles who minister in religious environments.

# The Meaning of "Church"

The idea of a church in the workplace is rooted in the meaning of the word "church." Most people think of "church" as a building for worship or a Christian service or a congregation with a pastor or an organized denomination. We commonly ask, for example, "Where do you go to church?" But what we usually think of as church today is not the full original biblical meaning.

The Greek word for church is *ekklesia*. In the first century when the Bible was written, the *ekklesia* was an assembly of the people convened for political purposes. However, in the New Testament the basic meaning of *ekklesia* becomes simply "the people of God." Wherever God's people are, there is the true church. Sometimes the people of God are gathered together in an assembly, and sometimes they are scattered throughout society. The New Testament uses *ekklesia* both ways, about half and half.

The tendency of Christian leaders throughout history has been to emphasize only the assembled people of God as being the real church. Some of this is based on stressing the political function of the ancient Greek *ekklesia*, as I have mentioned. True, the letters to the seven churches in Revelation 2 and 3 were written to the people of God assembled in certain places. But, on the other hand, check out the Book of Ephesians. Paul makes nine references to the church (*ekklesia*) in Ephesians, and not one of them signifies a church building or a geographical location or a specific congregation. They all refer to the people of God scattered out wherever they might be.

I'm belaboring this point because the recognition of a legitimate church in the workplace depends on it. Only if we follow the biblical pattern of the church being the people of God *both* gathered *and* scattered will the idea of the church in the workplace make any sense.

Our traditional thinking has been that the church meets one day a week, namely on Sundays. That, of course, is correct because on Sundays it is the church gathered. However, it is not the full story. Do the people of God who worship together on Sunday stop being the church the other six days of the week? Obviously not, because Monday through Saturday they are still the people of God, so logically they are just as much the true church as they were on Sunday. The one true church, then, has two different forms.

## The Nuclear Church and the Extended Church

What can we call these two different forms of the church? I think it is convenient to take our cue from sociology, which has distinguished the "nuclear family" from the "extended family." Most people are accustomed to this terminology. The nuclear family is those living under the same roof, ordinarily mother, father, and children. The extended family includes grandparents, aunts, uncles, cousins, in-laws, grandchildren, nephews, nieces, and the rest. It is all the same family, but taking two different and significant forms.

Why not call the two different forms of the church the "nuclear church" and the "extended church"? The nuclear church would be the people of God meeting in their congregation, whether in a church building or in a home. The extended church would be the people of God in the work-place, commonly called "the church in the workplace." In fact, one of my more recent books has as its title *The Church in the Workplace* (Regal Books).

## Biblical Government

Now, let's go back to biblical government. According to Ephe-sians 2:20, apostles and prophets constitute the operational foundation of the household of God, the church. If this is the case, there must be apostles and prophets (as well as evange-lists, pastors, and teachers) not only in the nuclear church, but in the extended church as well. Right now I'm concentrating on apostles, so one implication of what I have just said is that there must be such a thing as workplace (extended church) apostles. God has given them the spiritual gift of apostle, and He has called them to a ministry or activity in the workplace, as over against ministry in the nuclear church.

Just for perspective, this thought has only emerged in the Second Apostolic Age which, as I have said, began around 2001. Up until now almost all the literature on apostles and the New Apostolic Reformation assumed that apostles func-tioned only in the nuclear church. That was the case with my early books on apostles, I must admit. But God continually brings us to new levels and this is one of the newer ones. He gives us new wine and expects us to have new wineskins ready to receive it.

What does all this have to do with social transformation and taking dominion?

## Apostolic Spheres

Let's begin by looking at the concept of apostolic spheres. Inherent in the gift of apostle is extraordinary authority. So much so that the Bible says, *"God has appointed these in the church: first apostles"* (1 Cor. 12:28). Paul was one of them. Paul said, *"For even if I should boast somewhat more about our authority, which the Lord gave us for edification and not for your destruction, I shall not be ashamed"* (2 Cor. 10:8). However, Paul recognized that his apostolic authority was only effective within the spheres to which God had assigned him. That's why he says later in the same chapter, *"We, however, will not boast beyond measure, but within the limits of the sphere which God appointed us—a sphere which especially includes you"* (2 Cor. 10:13).

Paul knew, for example, that he did not have apostolic authority among the churches of Alexandria or the churches of Jerusalem or the churches of India where Thomas had gone. But he did have authority among the churches of Corinth and Ephesus and Galatia and Philippi because these were among the apostolic spheres to which God had assigned him.

## The 7-M Template

Now let's switch to the workplace. What are the major spheres of the workplace to which God might assign apostles? Everyone who is currently addressing issues relating to the area of faith at work recognizes that certain spheres exist. However, there is not yet full agreement on how many there are or what the spheres might be. I have seen lists as low as three spheres and as high as 113. There is a growing consensus, however, that we all agree on the "Seven Mountains" brought to our attention in the early 2000s by business consultant Lance Wallnau. Wallnau says, "If the world is to be won, these are the mountains that mold the culture and the minds of men. Whoever controls these mountains controls the direction of the world and the harvest therein."[1]

What are the Seven Mountains? They are the Religion Mountain, the Family Mountain, the Education Mountain, the Media Mountain, the Government Mountain, the Arts and Entertainment Mountain, and the Business Mountain. I have listed them in random order, not necessarily the order of importance. Obviously, each one of the seven could be subdivided any number of times. For example, the Business Mountain would include construction, shipping, health care, agriculture, engineering, insurance, mining, transportation, technology, retail, hotels, financial trading, and any number of other sub spheres. The other six mountains would have similar subdivisions. God's desire is that kingdom-minded people influence each one and impart the values of God's kingdom here on earth.

I found it fascinating to learn from Wallnau that these seven spheres of society can be traced back to two outstanding Christian leaders—Bill Bright, founder of Campus Crusade for Christ, and Loren Cunningham, founder of Youth with a Mission (YWAM). These two men reportedly first met each other at a luncheon. While they were eating, one of them listed off what he thought were the seven principal segments of society that must be brought under the headship of Christ. After he named them, the other reached into his pocket and, with a smile, pulled out a list he had prepared for that meeting. Amazingly, their lists, using slightly different terminology, were identical! They are what Wallnau has labeled the Seven Mountains.

Lance Wallnau would say that few, if any, outsiders could enter one of the Seven Mountains and expect to reach the top. They would need to be insiders. Why? Because each one of the Seven Mountains has a distinct culture.

## Culture Counts

Speaking of culture, many do not realize how wide the cultural gap is between the nuclear church and the church in the workplace. A remarkable scientific study on this was done a few years ago by Laura Nash of Harvard Business School and Scotty McLennan of Stanford University, financed by a grant from the Lily Endowment. They did not use the terms "nuclear church" and "extended church," but instead the title of their book is Church on Sunday, Work on Monday. They discovered that the cultural gap between the two is enormous. For example, Nash and McLennan say, "Businesspeople and clergy live in two worlds. Between the two groups lie minefields seeded with attitudes about money, poverty, and the spirit of business."[2]

The anthropological view is that human culture is simply a set of rules that provides certain values and behavior patterns, helping people in a given society to live together harmoniously and productively. Each culture has its own rule book, like, for example, American and Japanese culture. Americans eat with forks, keep their shoes on in the house, greet by shaking hands, and drive on the right. Japanese eat with chopsticks, take their shoes off before going in the house, greet by bowing, and drive on the left. Which is right and which is wrong? Anthropologists would say that both are right. American culture is right for America and Japanese culture is right for Japan.

Now, carry this over to the nuclear church and the extended church. As Nash and McLennan have shown, they each have different rule books. Most workplace believers understand both rule books. They live under one of them Monday through Saturday, and they are accustomed to switching to the other one on Sunday. However, here is the rub. Most nuclear church leaders understand only one rule book, namely their own, and they tend to think that much of the extended church rulebook is wrong! This obviously is a recipe for misunderstanding at best and conflict at worst. One of the most urgent tasks at hand is for all of us to continue to build bridges of recognition, trust, and appreciation between the two cultures.

## Bluegrass in Casinos

I feel that an important step toward building understanding between nuclear church leaders and extended church leaders is to know what the differing rules are as accurately as possible. With this in mind, I used Part 2 of my book The Church in the Workplace to unpack eight of the rules. They address issues such as time management and stewardship and the tough calls and pragmatism and others. To give one example, let me make reference to my friend, Ricky Skaggs, of country music and bluegrass fame. Ricky is a committed, Spirit-filled, humble, God-honoring believer. When not in church, he adheres to the rule book of the extended church.

Let's imagine a scenario in which the pastors of a city were among the leaders of an effort to stop a municipal initiative to allow casinos in the city. The initiative passed, however, and a casino moved in, much to the dismay of the pastors who saw the casino as a dangerous stronghold of darkness in their midst. Ricky Skaggs gets an invitation to bring his band and perform in the casino. The nuclear church rule book would tell him to turn it down and not use his God-given talents for the devil. But Ricky's extended church rule book sees things differently. He likens himself to King David of old, and he feels that God is directing him to use his instruments in a spiritual way to drive out demons and to usher in the Holy Spirit, so he accepts the invitation with the proviso that he gives his testimony as part of his performance.

Who is right and who is wrong? Each rule has a dimension of validity. Ideally, there should be mutual respect. The pastors should recognize Skaggs as a mature leader in the church in the workplace and a peer in ministry. Instead of scolding him (which, incidentally, many have done to Ricky in real life), they should respect his ability to hear from God and make the proper decision, even though they might not agree with it. As far as bluegrass in casinos is concerned, pastors are clearly outsiders, while Ricky Skaggs is a knowledgeable insider.

## The Seven Mountains

Think of Lance Wallnau's seven mountains. Each one of the seven mountains has a distinct culture as well. The culture of business is obviously different from the culture of government, which is different from the culture of education, and so on. True, there would be many commonalities across the mountains for those of us who live in America, but the differences are the crucial nuances for anyone attempting to go to the top and take dominion of one particular sphere. Although some might be able to manage it, very few people have the ability to function effectively in more than one of the cultures.

Let me illustrate this by citing an article written by Steven Sample, President of the University of Southern California. He is concerned that "We live in an age in which the disciplines that comprise the arts and humanities have become estranged from the disciplines of science and technology." He goes on to reference C.P. Snow who "described scientists and literary intellectuals as belonging to two cultures which were unable to communicate with each other."[3] Samples' worthy point is that USC is committed to building bridges between the two, but I was struck by the widespread recognition on the part of informed people of cultural gaps such as these in the real world.

This highlights a major reason why workplace apostles are absolutely essential for social transformation. Only apostles, whatever kind they might be, have the God-given authority to influence and take charge of a certain segment of society on behalf of the kingdom of God. This is true not only of all seven mountains, but also in each and every significant subdivision of the seven, such as arts and sciences as two subdivisions of education.

Where would nuclear church apostles have their strategic influence? Obviously in the Religion Mountain. No argument. But where else? Some would undoubtedly respond that they influence family as well. There is some truth to this. Even though they may not use the title, nuclear church apostles such as James Dobson and Donald Wildemon, as well as the Rick Warrens and the Bill Hybles and the Joel Osteens, have had a positive influence on the Family Mountain. However, many would argue that, here in America and in our lifetimes, the media unfortunately has had considerably more influence on the American family than the church. Few would disagree.

Let's give them the benefit of the doubt and agree that nuclear church apostles can influence one and a half of the seven mountains. That leaves five and a half crucial mountains in which nuclear church apostles have virtually no influence whatsoever. That's why we cannot depend on nuclear church apostles alone to lead the charge for taking dominion. It will not happen without workplace apostles filled with the Holy Spirit and intent on serving God by taking dominion of whatever mountain or subdivision thereof in which God has placed them.

## Setting Things in Order

A major function of apostles is to set things in order (see Tit. 1:5). Apostles see the big picture. They are purpose-driven. They grasp the task at hand and they figure out ways to get it done. They cast vision. They locate and utilize the needed material and human resources. They are motivators. People recognize their authority, respect their leadership, and willingly join the team, contributing what they can to accomplish the goals.

Now, think of the average workplace. Chances are that there will be a number of Christians there. Just about all of them will know that they are supposed to be salt and light in their workplace because they have learned that in church. Most of them have tried their best to influence their workplace for God. However, they have been doing this for maybe five or ten or fifteen years, and nothing has changed. In some cases, things have become worse! What is going on? They pray. They witness for Christ. They live moral lives. They do their job well. They make friends with others. They exhibit the fruit of the Spirit. Many, understandably, become discouraged and begin to believe that nothing will ever change. Talk about taking dominion can seem very unrealistic at times.

## Overthrowing a Government

I have a suggestion. I think that what may well be lacking in the typical workplace scenario I have just described is simply a government. Let's remember that our responsibility for taking dominion amounts to an invasion of territory that satan has been holding for a long time. Think of the seven mountains. Satan has succeeded in maintaining control in most of them because he has established a government in each one. And it takes a government to overthrow a government. The people of God constitute the church in the workplace, but it has been relatively impotent because it does not have a biblical government. In a word, the workplace apostles have not been activated.

I say "activated" because I think the apostles are already there in the workplace. God has taken the responsibility to gift and call those whom He has chosen to be apostles, prophets, evangelists, pastors, and teachers. But those who are so gifted need to be recognized, encouraged, and even commissioned if they are going to be properly activated. We do this in the nuclear church fairly well, but we are still a bit deficient when it comes to the extended church.

One of the reasons why it has been so difficult for us is that most of us have never thought this way before. Take, for example, John Maxwell, one of the top-ranking teachers on leadership in our nation. He sees the big picture because while he spent most of his career as a nuclear church leader, the last few years have drawn him into the workplace, I dare say functioning as a workplace apostle. Reviewing the past, Maxwell admits that "one of my major mistakes was thinking that life revolved around the local church and what we were doing. For example, if you were a member of the church, you had to have a ministry in the church."[4] He goes on to say, "I had a lot of high-capacity people who were probably never 'salt and light' like they could have been. I'd change that immediately if I went back to the local church. I'd be much more into how we influenced the community and a lot less into 'How can I get everybody on board with my church and my program.'"[5] I wish that every nuclear church leader would move into this new kind of thinking.

It is, of course, important to every believer in the workplace where they go to their nuclear church on Sunday. In a given workplace we might well find Presbyterians, Nazarenes,

Lutherans, Assemblies of God, Salvation Army, Baptists, Apostolics, Mennonites, and many others. Their denominational identity would be important to them on Sunday, but simply being a Christian who desires to make a difference is all that counts Monday through Saturday.

Let's assume that all the believers in this workplace want to be salt and light, but that they lack a government. How could this government be established? It is very unlikely that a viable government could be provided by a nuclear church leader coming in from the outside mainly because of the traditional religious baggage that each one would bring. Furthermore, most nuclear church apostles don't even begin to understand the culture or the rule book of the workplace. On the other hand, if it is a workplace apostle, they usually don't carry much religious baggage and operating in the culture and rule book of the workplace comes naturally. Consequently, workplace apostles, not nuclear church apostles, are the ones who would have the best potential to establish a government that can transform that segment of society.

## Territorial Spheres

Up to this point I have been focusing the potential influence of workplace apostles on the seven mountains. Each of the seven mountains need apostolic government if the forces of darkness are going to be pushed back. But let's go beyond that. When we think of "transforming society," the word "society" usually means a collection of people living together in a certain geographical region like a neighborhood, a community, a city, a province, or even a nation.

For example, in Chapter 2 I described the city of Almolonga, Guatemala as a sociologically verifiable case study of social transformation. At this writing, at least to my knowledge, it is the only significant social unit that has been transformed, in the past tense. However, George Otis, Jr. has identified over 500 cities and other social units that are currently quite advanced in the process toward social transformation. Some of them will make it to verifiable transformation, others will stall out, and still others will regress over time.

One of the major variables will undoubtedly be the government that God's people are able to establish in order to confront the government of darkness over the geographical territories in which satan has long since been entrenched. In most cases this will require on-site apostolic leadership. In Almolonga, several apostles emerged to lead the transformation of the city. One of the best known has been Mariano Riscajche who is a member of the International Coalition of Apostles (ICA). He began the process by casting out numerous demons of alcoholism, and he then grew a megachurch with its facility right on the central plaza of the city. He helped establish a government of righteousness that succeeded in pushing satan's government out of the territory.

In Riscajche's case, God soon expanded his territorial assignment, not just to the city but to the nations. It was prophesied that Almolonga would be a light to the nations and Riscajche, now based in California, is traveling internationally with signs and wonders accompanying him. In one season he was a territorial apostle, but now in a new season his apostolic mantle is a blessing everywhere. Keep in mind that, at this writing, Almolonga is the only city that has passed the test of sociologically verifiable transformation.

The idea of territories as apostolic spheres is biblical. When I explained apostolic spheres a while ago, I mentioned that Paul had apostolic authority in Corinth and Ephesus (Asia) and Philippi and Galatia, but not in Alexandria or Jerusalem or India.

With this in mind, it would be accurate to refer to Paul as a territorial apostle in those regions within his spheres. Peter also is very specific about his assigned territories: Pontus, Galatia, Cappadocia, Asia, and Bithynia (see 1 Pet. 1:1). It is interesting to note that both Paul and Peter had territorial apostolic influence in Asia and Galatia. However, even though their territories overlapped, their ministries and spheres of authority did not because Paul was an apostle to the uncircumcision, the Gentiles, while Peter was an apostle to the circumcision, the Jews.

## Persevering Leadership

The first of five commonalities that George Otis, Jr. has identified in cities and regions well along the process toward social transformation is "persevering leadership."[6] What kind of leadership would we expect? If what I have been saying is correct, it must be nothing less than apostolic leadership.

Let's not confuse apostolic leadership with pastoral leadership. I say this because I am among those who made the serious mistake of confusing the two a few years ago. As I have pointed out, the notion of social transformation only began to appear on the radar screens of us charismatically inclined evangelicals in 1990 with the publication of John Dawson's *Taking Our Cities for God*. As many of us began to strategize ways and means of making this happen, we agreed with George Otis, Jr. that persevering leadership would be essential. During the 1990s the office of apostle was just beginning to be recognized, but still by only a few. The most prominent Christian leadership that we knew of across the board was local church pastors.

In an effort to define some sort of a spiritual government in our cities, we developed the idea of "the church of the city." This meant that in a given city there was only one Christian church made up of many congregations, and that the pastors of the local churches were to be regarded as "co-pastors" of the church of the city. We started labeling the local church pastors "the spiritual gatekeepers of the city." This sounded good and it seemed quite biblical, but it had a serious flaw. It unintentionally ended up neutralizing strong leadership. Why? Because if all the pastors were "co-pastors," they all had equal voice in what happened in the city. That meant that the losers would have as much influence as the winners. Make no mistake about it, in any given city some pastors are losers and others are winners. If the winners are not in charge, city transformation cannot and will not happen.

Now that we are in the Second Apostolic Age, we recognize that pastors are not the spiritual gatekeepers of the city as we once thought. Apostles, more specifically *territorial* apostles, must be seen as the spiritual gatekeepers of the city. Some of these territorial apostles will emerge from the nuclear church, most likely certain megachurch pastors, but I am convinced that the great majority of them will come from the extended church. Our workplace apostles have the greatest potential for leading the forces for city transformation. They are the ones most deeply embedded in the six non-Religion Mountains. They are winners. They know how to make things happen once they are given the opportunity.

It would be difficult, if not impossible, to imagine taking dominion back from satan without the active participation of the church in the workplace. I realize that this a fairly new thought, and that the practical implementation of these principles is still in the beginning stages. We are identifying workplace apostles, an essential first step. Among the 500 members of the International Coalition of Apostles (ICA) at this writing, some 60 to 70 are listed as workplace or extended church apostles. However, this is not to say that they have been activated and strategically deployed to anyone's satisfaction. The day is soon coming, however, when these generals of God will more and more be fulfilling their destiny for extending His kingdom.

# Chapter 8

# A NEW STRATEGY: LEARNING FROM EXPERIENCE

Why do we need to talk about a new strategy? Simply because, up to now, the strategies for social transformation that we have been experimenting with have not worked as well as we might have hoped. We have been trying and trying and trying. We have seen many encouraging signs. But transformation? Our quivers have not yet been filled with stories of human societies having been transformed and that transformation subsequently being sustained. God's kingdom is yet to come on earth as it is in heaven.

## Clarifying Our Goals

The first step toward determining a strategy is to have a viable goal. The goal, of course, is what counts. The strategy is only a means to accomplish the end. The reason I mention this is that somehow a large number of people have been programmed with the ridiculous notion that "the end doesn't justify the means." It will not require much hard thinking to realize that nothing at all can possibly justify the means except the end. What would be the use of developing a strategy (the means) if you do not first know what the goal (the end) is?

Some will respond that we cannot use immoral means to accomplish a given end, even though it might be a moral end. This, of course, is true. Let's agree, therefore, that we must be ethical in everything we do. Having agreed on that up front, I suggest that we now move out of the realm of ethics and into the realm of practical strategy.

There will always be more than one ethically neutral option for a strategy, so which option do we choose? We naturally choose the strategy that will best accomplish the goal. Another way of saying this is "Do whatever it takes!" This line of thinking predictably surfaces the related issue of pragmatism. For whatever reason, "pragmatism," in the minds of large numbers of nuclear church leaders, is regarded as little short of transgression. Pious phrases like "What really matters is who I am, not what I do," or "The process is more important than the outcome," or "God knows that my heart is right," are geared toward opening the door for comfortably rationalizing lack of success in a given project.

In my opinion, these two naïve assumptions on the part of many Christian leaders have short-circuited the accomplishment of large numbers of efforts toward improving society. Those who do not understand the relationship of the means to the end or those who have a knee-jerk aversion to pragmatism are generally those who are satisfied with intentions rather than insisting on production. For them, carefully defining goals is something we can put off until we have more time. Such people tend to become nervous when someone suggests establishing objective measuring devices to evaluate progress toward a certain goal.

## Accomplishing Our Goals

Needless to say, I have always been a person who values pragmatism. This, I know, has cost me some friendships. For example, one of my self-perceived badges of honor is to have had a whole book written to criticize my (and George Barna's) pragmatism![1] What the book said about me was true! So because I am pragmatic and because I want to see my goals accomplished, three things become extremely important to me:

- A clear and precise definition of our goal
- The most efficient strategy to accomplish that goal
- A measuring device to gauge and evaluate the progress being made

Too many of our recent Christian efforts toward fulfilling the cultural mandate have lacked these three elements and consequently have not lived up to our expectations. As I mentioned in a previous chapter, one of our more outstanding leaders who has spent decades developing principles and practices of transformational development is Bryant Myers. Myers, formerly of World Vision International and now with Fuller Seminary, is one who would agree with the three elements I have listed. His book *Walking with the Poor* is a thoughtful analysis of what has been done in the past and what needs to be done in the future.

Myers says that our strategy must include "learning our way into the future."[2] This requires constant measurement and evaluation. Our goal becomes a "marker on the horizon."[3] Then he says, "However much off course our short-term work ends up, regular evaluations allow us to know where we are in terms of where we want to go. With a clear vision and values, we can now work on short-term plans, stopping periodically to see if where we ended up is directed toward our vision. If it is, we plan another step and evaluate again. If it is not, then we redirect our plan, take another short-term step, and evaluate again."[4] Like the term or not, this is a pragmatic approach.

## Our Marker: City Transformation

Obviously the first step is to determine what marker we are going to plant on the horizon. The whole thesis of this book is that our ultimate goal should be God's mandate for His people to retake the dominion over creation that Adam forfeited to satan in the Garden of Eden. This means that our marker is nothing short of social transformation.

Our long range, our vision is to see all human life on planet Earth enjoying the values and the blessings of the kingdom of God. But this, of course, is not going to happen all at once. Consequently, we need to start with smaller, more manageable social units. We could strategically think of our neighborhood or our town or our city or our region or our state or our nation. We could think of the "seven mountains" that I described in Chapter 7 and what it would be like to transform the business mountain or the education mountain or the media mountain or the government mountain. We could think of transforming our own corporation or the construction industry or health care.

This is just a matter of opinion, but I believe that the most viable social unit across the board toward which we should initially direct our strategies is the city. As a starter, this reflects the title of John Dawson's landmark book which I have referred to several times, *Taking Our Cities for God.* Cities are recognized, well-defined, manageable units of society. Therefore, when I think about setting up a marker on the horizon to establish our goal, I am mostly referring to the transformation of our cities. I realize that the Bible tells us to make disciples of "nations" (see Matt. 28:19-20), but powerful first steps toward that goal would be to make disciples of the cities of a particular nation. The cities usually constitute the strategic power centers of a nation.

## When Is It Done?

If the transformation of a city is our marker, how do we know if and when we have accomplished that goal? I raise this question because over the last few years quite a number of Christian leaders in many places have become involved in trying to make things like this happen. However, with the exception of Almolonga, Guatemala, it has been difficult to identify a truly transformed city. By "transformed," as I suggested in Chapter 2, I mean sociologically verifiable transformation. This would require an independent investigator, who is qualified to assess situations like this, issuing a public statement that the city has indeed been authentically transformed. Such a thing, for example, was done with Almolonga. In that case it was an investigative journalist who researched what had happened and published his findings in Crónica Semanal, the Guatemalan equivalent of Time magazine.

The reason we need an outsider to do this is that many church leaders, in well-intentioned efforts to encourage those who may be supporting them in one way or another, have shown a tendency toward exaggerating the importance of anecdotes. They sometimes celebrate abortion clinics shutting down or lower crime rates or a nativity scene in front of city hall or a major drug bust or a believer elected as mayor or a drought being broken or similar good reports as indications that the city has been transformed. These might be legitimate signs that a transformation process is indeed under way in a given city, but they fall short of sociologically verifiable transformation.

Here is how Bryant Myers sees it: "The underlying theological frame is that God has created a good and life-giving social world; wherever we find good in our world, we are seeing evidence of God's work and gifts. The biblical story is the account of God's project to restore the lives of individuals and communities, marred by sin, so that they can be good, just, and peaceful once again."[5] When this happens to a city, we can say it has been transformed.

## Phase Three

As I said in the beginning of this chapter, the reason we need to consider a new strategy is that the strategies we have been attempting haven't been working as well as we might have desired. It would be nice if a city or two other than Almolonga would join the ranks of verifiably transformed cities. Possibly Usinsk in Russia also qualifies. When we add other cities to the list, we will naturally highlight the strategies that made it happen and see what we can do toward applying them in other cities.

Some might interpret history differently, but I would like to suggest that we are moving into Phase Three of God's unfolding plan among evangelicals to take dominion. My desire is that this book would at least provide some valuable pieces toward drafting a blueprint for Phase Three. I am focusing on "evangelicals" in the broad sense of the term because worldwide, according to researchers like David Barrett and Philip Jenkins, evangelicals, and especially charismatically inclined evangelicals, represent the huge bulk of today's living body of Christ, which will continue to be on the cutting edge for generations to come.

I see Phase One as the "social action phase." When I summarized the history of the social transformation movement in Chapter 2, I suggested that this phase began with Lausanne 1974. This is when many evangelicals began getting on board with the cultural mandate. Previously, Christian social ministries had largely been co-opted by the Social Gospel Movement, which did not include evangelicals because it had deemphasized or even rejected the evangelistic mandate. Phase One evangelicals began to stress caring for the poor and disadvantaged. They supported causes such as social justice, national righteousness, liberation rather than oppression, racial equality, equitable distribution of wealth, education, health care, and ecological improvement while at the same time saving souls and multiplying churches.

Having said this, strategies for social transformation as we have been defining it were not a prominent part of Phase One. Dominion theology had not appeared on the agendas of most social action evangelicals. In fact, when the issue did come up it was frequently dismissed as a defective theology pointing toward theocracy, a notion often derided as "triumphalism." Advocates of dominion theology were sternly warned against sliding back into Constantinianism. I would guess that Phase One lasted about 16 years, 1974–1989.

Phase Two, as I have said, was kicked off by John Dawson's *Taking Our Cities for God*. The book's title itself reflects the goal of social transformation. The strategies applied at the time revolved largely around a set of relatively new concepts of strategic-level spiritual warfare and associated activities, which I detailed in Chapter 6. A crucial part of Phase Two was the beginning of progressive revelation concerning the biblical government of the church, which I dealt with in Chapter 2. Some more explicit views of dominion theology began surfacing at this time, but they were largely kept in the background. Phase Two also lasted around 16 years, 1990–2006.

## Transformation Fatigue

During Phase Two, the "city-taking" phase, some transformation fatigue seemed to be setting in. The fact that we had been working with our top charismatically inclined evangelical leadership in virtually every city in America for 16 years, but that we could not yet point to a single transformed city in our nation, would tend to be discouraging. By way of analysis, four possible explanations for this could be offered:

1. We had the wrong goal. It is too much to expect that whole cities can be transformed. I disagree. I think we have been tuning into God's true mandate.

2. We have the right goal, but we have taken the wrong approach. We must do something different. I disagree. I think that what we have been doing has been very good.

3. We are taking the right approach, but we have not done it enough. Let's do the same for 16 more years. I disagree. No more status quo. Something needs to be changed.

4. What we have been doing is fine, but it is incomplete. I agree with this explanation. I believe we need to add fresh strategy to what we have already received from God. I couldn't have written this book during Phase Two, but God continues to give us new wine, and I believe we will faithfully develop the necessary new wineskins in Phase Three.

## It Can Be Done!

One of the reasons I am convinced that cities can be transformed is that we have some concrete examples, although admittedly not in the U.S. I have mentioned Almolonga,

Guatemala and Usinsk, Russia. I hope that there are other examples of which I am not aware.

To show that it can be done, I love to go back in history to Florence, Italy, where Girolamo Savanarola led a notable example of transformation. I have told the story in other books, but it is so encouraging that I want to repeat it again:

> The wicked city government [of Florence] was overthrown, and Savanarola taught the people to set up a democratic form of government. The revival brought tremendous moral change. The people stopped reading vile and worldly books. Merchants made restitution to the people for the excessive profits they had been making. Hoodlums and street urchins stopped singing sinful songs and began to sing hymns in the streets. Carnivals were forbidden and forsaken.
>
> Huge bonfires were made of worldly books and obscene pictures, masks, and wigs.
>
> ...A great octagonal pyramid of worldly objects was erected in the public square of Florence. It towered in seven stages sixty feet high and 240 feet in circumference. While bells tolled, the people sang hymns and the fires burned.[6]

Adding one more contemporary example, let's go to Cambodia where Morris Ruddick tells this fascinating story:

> Almost a decade ago, I was struck by an alliance between a successful Christian entrepreneur and a seasoned missionary. [Note the connection of

a nuclear church leader and an extended church leader—ed.] They had banded together to mobilize a small group of Christians in an impoverished Buddhist village in rural Cambodia. Work was scarce and the majority in this village had barely enough to feed their families one meal a day.

With an ample supply of clay from the surrounding soil, they launched a simple business that created decorative clay pots, designed as wall-hangers. Distribution was found though United Kingdom gift shops. The demand for the clay pots began increasing, and soon this handful of Cambodian Christians began hiring others from their village as their business expanded. As this enterprise grew, more and more families started eating two and then three meals a day! The owners shared with their workers the truths about Jesus and the principles of God's word. Over time the result was that hunger was alleviated and the entire village embraced the goodness of the Lord and became Christians.

Now villagers are visiting other villages with the Good News.[7]

## Learning from Experience

It is one thing to recognize that city transformation is possible, but it is another thing to develop a strategy that can be transferred from one situation to another. I wish that I could produce what scientists call a "proof of principle experiment," which is the link between theory and practice. But the only way that a proof of principle experiment can become a reality is through laborious trial and error. Benjamin Franklin, for example, failed and failed again before he was able to harness electricity. However, he could never have even begun the process without a theory in mind. Once he went to work, each failure became a positive step along the road because he was continually discovering how it could not be done. He understood how to learn from experience.

As I set out to write this book on taking dominion, I knew from the outset that I would be limited mostly to the theory part. I have great hope that one of these days we will have multiple reports of successful, sociologically verifiable projects that have transformed numerous cities for the kingdom of God. But we do not have them as yet. We do have numbers of promising efforts in process and some of these will undoubtedly prove to be successful. Currently the most complete catalog of these efforts is found in Rick Heeren's *Extraordinary Miracles* (Regal Books). Additionally, toward the end of this chapter I will highlight what might prove to be our most viable guidelines for a new strategy of social transformation suggested by a workplace apostle, Ken Eldred.

## The Dream for Africa

When Bruce Wilkinson's *Prayer of Jabez* became an unexpected, runaway bestseller in 2000, Wilkinson began casting a vision to use his new-found wealth and celebrity status for a massive project of social transformation. Disappointingly, in less than four years it had taken a nosedive from which it could not recover. Despite constantly praying, *"Oh, that You would bless me indeed, and enlarge my territory"* (1 Chron. 4:10), Wilkinson, unlike Jabez, did not see his prayer answered. When, in 2005, he announced his abrupt resignation from his high-profile ministry, Dream for Africa, Wilkinson said, "Somewhere in this it's got to be all right to attempt a vision that didn't work and not to make it an overwhelming failure."[8]

One of the ways to keep Dream for Africa from entering mission history as a total failure is to learn from it what not to do in future transformation-oriented projects. Benjamin Franklin had his failures as well, but he kept learning from experience.

What did Bruce Wilkinson attempt? On his visits to Africa through the years, God had given him a burden for Africa's 20 million orphans, most of them a result of their parents' dying of AIDS. His two targets became care for orphans and prevention of AIDS, as well as the underlying poverty. While Dream for Africa targeted the whole continent, Wilkinson chose as his pilot project the impoverished nation of Swaziland, adjacent to South Africa, with a population of less than Phoenix, Arizona. Swaziland, with 70,000 orphans, is dealing with over 40 percent of its adult population infected with the AIDS virus. Most of its citizens make less than $1.00 per day.

## The Dream Village Tourist Attraction

Wilkinson thought he had the king's permission to build an "African Dream Village," which would house 10,000 orphans with Swazi supervisors as well as providing the site for a tourist attraction with an airport, a luxury hotel, a golf course, and a base for African safaris. He envisioned American donors, who wished to combine charity with an African vacation, filling the hotel. In order to enhance the safaris, he asked the government to grant him control of the nation's two best game reserves. He planned a "Mega Farm," plus some industries that hopefully would make the Dream Village self-sustaining. To combat AIDS, he launched a program with American volunteers on short term missions, to promote sexual abstinence in Swaziland's 172 high schools.

As it turns out, Wilkinson's most damaging mistake was his missiological naïveté. With little field experience in cross-cultural communication, he was perceived by many within and without Swaziland as a stereotypical ugly American. He was even warned by U.S. Ambassador Lewis Lucke that the plan to move orphans from their native villages to the African Dream Village would be a serious violation of Swazi cultural norms, but the warning went unheeded. The Swazi media picked this up and an editor for the *Swazi News* wrote, "Why can't [Wilkinson] simply tell us that he wants to be given the whole country so that he can gloat to his friends overseas that he owns a modern day colony in Africa called Swaziland?"[9]

Unicef in Swaziland turned against him. The breaking point came when Wilkinson realized that he had made the cultural error of misunderstanding the king. While the king had been exhibiting appropriate African courtesy to a well-known and well-heeled American visitor, he apparently never had any intention of agreeing with or supporting the African Dream Village.

## Guatemala's Ríos Montt

One might suspect that if the Swazi king (who, by the way, has 13 wives) had been a committed, born-again believer, Bruce Wilkinson's project might have fared better. Not necessarily. I recall the elation among U.S. Christian leaders when Efraín Ríos Montt became Guatemala's first born-again president back in the early 1980s. He had a noble vision of ending corruption and overcoming the Marxist guerilla bands that were ravaging the nation. The U.S. evangelical media, including Charisma, Christianity Today, Pat Robertson's CBN, Jerry Falwell, Luis Palau, and others raised hopes of authentic social transformation of that nation. Palau said, "The hand of God appears to be on him."[10]

However, under Ríos Montt's regime the violence in Guatemala reached unprecedented heights with some 200,000 fatalities, mostly among innocent, civilian indigenous peoples. He undoubtedly was up against high-level spiritual forces of evil who were having their way. Despite all his good intentions, he could not control his own military and after only 17 months in office, he was deposed by a coup. Transformation did not happen despite the backing of the international body of Christ and influence at the highest government level. There must be a better strategy, and I think it will relate to taking dominion of all seven mountains, not just one or two.

## Sustainability

Many of the well-intentioned efforts toward social transformation have turned out to be flashes in the pan. Some encouraging stories and anecdotes have been reported, but they are a far cry from sociologically verifiable transformation. Bryant Myers identifies one of the chief issues as sustainability. Here is the way he puts it:

> There have been too many examples in the past of development programming that seemed to be making a difference as long as the staff and the money of the development agency were present. Program evaluations, performed after the money and staff were withdrawn, revealed that the entire development enterprise had proven more than the community could sustain on its own. Within a year or two, it was hard to find evidence that there had been a program at all. In some cases, things actually got worse because the community had become dependent on external sources and now suffered from diminished capacity.[11]

This means that when we launch efforts toward social transformation it is just as important to scope out the long-range implications as it is to alleviate the immediate situation by feeding the hungry and clothing the naked. I repeat, our social transformation projects have a better chance of being sustained if we simultaneously target all seven molders of culture.

## Afghan Opium

An interesting case at hand in Afghanistan shows how a short-term victory can quickly be turned around by the forces of evil to maintain satan's dominion over a society.

The U.S.-led war against the Taliban in Afghanistan seemed like it would produce positive social transformation when the Taliban was finally toppled in 2001. However, unforeseen developments have dimmed the prospects for sustainability. Why? Under the Taliban, growing poppies for opium production was outlawed. By 2000 the crop had all but disappeared. However, once the Taliban had been driven into the mountains their anti-government strategy became the opposite. The warlords set out to encourage opium production by offering military protection (for a price) to the farmers, and they have been successful. The previous record before the Taliban crackdown was 4,600 metric tons of opium in 1999, but by 2006 the harvest had reached around 6,100 metric tons, a 49 percent increase! Millions of dollars spent by the international community to fight production of the drug have been of no avail. Afghan opium now provides around 90 percent of the world's consumption of heroin!

Social transformation? By 2006 the Bush administration had "expressed concern that Afghanistan was in danger of becoming a full-fledged 'narcotics state,' where drug lords call the shots in governing the country."[12]

## Warren's P.E.A.C.E. Plan

Bruce Wilkinson is not the only bestselling Christian author with a vision to use his newly acquired wealth to transform society. Rick Warren, author of The Purpose-Driven Life, is another. Instead of Swaziland, Warren has chosen Rwanda as his target social unit. Learning from Wilkerson's failure to do so, Warren did establish firm personal relationships with Rwandan president Paul Kagame. In 2005 they jointly announced their venture to make Rwanda the "world's first purpose-driven nation."[13]

Warren's strategy is to address the five "global giants" that plague society worldwide, namely spiritual emptiness, egocentric leadership, poverty, disease, and illiteracy. His acronym for this is "P.E.A.C.E.:"

- Plant (or partner with) churches
- Equip leaders
- Assist the poor
- Care for the sick
- Educate the next generation

At this writing it is too early to begin to assess the results of the P.E.A.C.E. plan or to predict whether it will result in sociologically verifiable transformation of Rwanda. I mention it, however, because it has created unprecedented enthusiasm among Christian leaders and churches in America. Many are convinced that it will be more productive than past attempts. One observer, for example, says, "The P.E.A.C.E. plan is different because it has an integrated strategy...[Their leaders] are approaching their work in a much more holistic fashion than we have seen realized in the past. It integrates not only across the spectrum of human needs, but also across the spectrum of resources."[14]

Although admittedly it is a risk at this early stage, some observations might be in order. I would think that the P.E.A.C.E. plan fits most comfortably into Phase One, the "social action" phase of strategies for obeying God's cultural mandate. The Phase Two emphases on strategic-level spiritual warfare and associated activities have not been placed front and center. Crucial to Phase Three, as I am defining it, are such things as the apostolic/prophetic government of the church, the church (including apostles) in the workplace, the great transfer of wealth, and dominion theology. My feeling is that, without all of the above, efforts to improve society will have many positive, but possibly short-term, effects. I could be wrong.

Let me suggest a couple of more radical strategic approaches, both of which are reportedly part of the long-range P.E.A.C.E. plan, although they haven't been made as explicit as the other features.

## Caring for the Sick

Let's begin with "caring for the sick." This is certainly necessary. In Africa, HIV/AIDS is the most massive challenge. As much as possible we need to show compassion to those infected through medications, treatment, hospitals, nutrition, hospice care, and support of family members, especially orphans. We need to take steps toward prevention through education, research toward producing vaccines, abstinence from sex outside of marriage, use of condoms, cleanliness, and hygiene. No one I know of, including Bill Gates, would refuse to support such positive measures.

But could we dream one step further? The first suggestion I heard for this came from my friend Ralph Winter of the U.S. Center for World Mission. Winter believes that the

HIV virus was probably not in God's original plan for human-kind. Could we postulate that it might have been introduced by satan after he usurped dominion of creation from Adam? If we are literally to see God's will done on earth as it is in heaven, it would be hard to imagine that the HIV virus would be alive and well in heaven. Perhaps our radical dominion mandate could include overcoming and eliminating the HIV virus itself so that it no longer even exists here on earth. If this makes sense, it would also make sense to extend the principle to causes of cancer and Alzheimer's and diabetes and heart disease and multiple sclerosis and even the common cold. Instead of "caring for the sick" we could possibly set as our ultimate goal "eliminating sickness"!

## Assisting the Poor

I have a similar thought concerning "assisting the poor." In numerous places, the Bible commands us to do this. I do not think that we will enjoy the blessing of God on any of our outreach ministries if we fail to assist the poor. A large percentage of Christians here in America welcome the opportunity to support organizations such as World Vision and Compassion International and the Samaritan's Purse and the Salvation Army, just to name a few. The more poor people in Rwanda that the P.E.A.C.E. plan can assist the better!

But could we dream one step further? Ed Silvoso of Harvest Evangelism was the first one from whom I heard the concept of uprooting "systemic poverty." Silvoso says, "Nation transformation must be tangible, and the premier social indicator is the elimination of systemic poverty."[15] This, again, sounds like the dominion mandate. God did not create Adam and Eve to live in poverty. Silvoso goes on to say, "In the Garden scene, in Genesis 3, we see that poverty became the first visible sign of deterioration in the Garden, as illustrated by the thorns and thistles and the land's lack of cooperation in yielding plentiful fruit."[16] Consequently poverty, like disease germs, must be an invention of satan who usurped Adam's dominion. Poverty, according to this view, is not something to be tolerated or merely reduced, but something that must be eliminated from a society that is truly transformed. It can be done. Check out Almolonga, which I have mentioned several times. Instead of "assisting the poor," we could set as our ultimate goal "eliminating systemic poverty."

## Some Roots of Systemic Poverty

A strategic step toward this is suggested by Andrew Paquin in his commentary on the P.E.A.C.E. plan. He cites Warren's calculation that Rwanda has the realistic potential to produce more quality fruit than the nation could consume. If the nation began to export fruit, some of the causes of systemic poverty could be reduced. But Paquin directs our attention to a larger international factor that may also be contributing to Rwanda's systemic poverty. It resides in the "consumer powerhouses of the West." He points out that "Currently the U.S. and the E.U. provide more than $90 billion in annual subsidies to their domestic agricultural producers in order to protect them against competition from foreign exporters."[17] The upshot is that spurring Rwandan agricultural production is a good first step, but the overall strategy must be accompanied by such things as changes in the structure of international trade if the roots of systemic poverty are to be totally pulled out.

Closer to home, we could consider the strategies to combat systemic poverty in the United States that Kansas Senator Samuel Brownback has proposed. He points out that the U.S. war on poverty began in 1965 when the poor were about 12 percent of the population. Since then the U.S. has spent no less than $3 trillion on alleviating systemic poverty. The results? The poor still comprise 12 percent of the population! Brownback's comment is the following: "The key to ending poverty, really, is getting at least a minimal education, getting married, not having children until you are married, and keeping the child. The number of people in poverty that have done those four basic things is very, very small."[18] While food stamps help temporarily, these basic principles go to the roots. Without them, poverty will persist.

## Business as Strategy

As I have said more than once, I do not believe we will be able to develop or implement an effective strategy for taking dominion without guidance from the leaders of what I have been calling "the church in the workplace." For the most part, nuclear church leaders have been directing our efforts in Phase One and Phase Two, but I am convinced that the new direction of Phase Three will largely come from extended church leaders.

A quite convincing argument for this has come from successful businessman Ken Eldred. The title of his book is revealing: *God Is at Work: Transforming People and Nations Through Business*. Eldred starts by providing a very perceptive analysis of our traditional, nuclear church-based paradigm of missions from the perspective of what I would describe as an extended church (workplace) apostle. While he is not hostile to the past, he casts a radically different vision for Phase Three.

Eldred believes that we need "an alternative missions strategy to the one of the past two centuries that relies on fully supported foreign missionaries."[19] He goes on to affirm that "traditional missionary church planters, evangelists, doctors, nurses, teachers and translators will always be important components of world missions. Any emerging missions movement like kingdom business must be complimentary to these. But," he says, "the traditional full-support missionary model will continue to face increasing pressure."[20]

## Workplace Missionaries

Essentially, Eldred's alternative strategy involves a shift from depending almost entirely on nuclear church missionaries to regarding international business people as legitimate Christian missionaries in their own right and entrusting them to lead us into the next phase of social transformation. He says, "I expect that Kingdom business will be a primary tool that revolutionizes missions in the twenty-first century by providing an economically self-sustaining vehicle that will enable an increasing number of missionary Christians to be welcome in any country."[21]

Certainly, as I have previously suggested, only workplace apostles have the street savvy to lead God's people into taking dominion of all seven mountains in any society.

And I agree that the overriding need in the least Christian nations of the world is for economic development, and that "the opportunity is ripe for missionary business people to take the gospel to nations all over the world."[22]

# Chapter 9

# A NEW INFLUENCE: MONEY ANSWERS EVERYTHING!

If you check back through human history, you will find that three things, more than anything else, have produced social transformation—namely violence, knowledge, and wealth. And the greatest of these is wealth!

Perhaps that is what Solomon had in mind when he wrote, *"Money answers everything"* (Eccl. 10:19)! In all likelihood, this is a figure of speech, but at the same time it reflects a very important principle.

You will recall that in the graphic on social transformation that I have displayed several times, one of the two pillars supporting "Social Transformation" is "The Great Transfer of Wealth." I am convinced that a significant reason why we have not yet taken any of our American cities for God is that we have not had enough money at our disposal. John Kelly and Paul Costa say, "There is no doubt that if the Kingdom of God is going to be established on earth, it is going to take a lot more money than the church has at present."[1]

We are getting more serious than ever in our commitment to make disciples of all nations. God's dominion mandate tells us that, by the power of the Holy Spirit, His people must replace satan's dominion over the nations with the blessings of the kingdom of God. If this is to happen, an essential part of the process should be to transfer the control of wealth. As long as those who are pleasing satan remain in charge of the economy of the world, we can expect little progress. Now that we are in the Second Apostolic Age, however, I believe that we need to be prepared for some radical changes.

## Buying a Nation?

Not long ago, for example, I was ministering to some apostles in South Africa. One of them, a black South African probably in his 40s, asked me a question that was shocking. He said, "Peter, would you like to buy a nation?" Since I had never heard such a question and I was curious to see where it would lead, I quickly replied, "Yes! What country? What would it take?"

He explained to me that he had been building relationships with apostles in the Democratic Republic of the Congo. The Congo was arguably the most miserable nation in Africa. It had not seen an election in decades. It had been tyrannized by dictators and warlords who were driven by greed and a lust for power with no hint of compassion for the welfare of the people they ruled. Top-level African leaders had all but given up on the nation. But changes were on the horizon. A democratic election had been scheduled.

My friend told me that the apostolic movement in the Congo had, for the first time in history, achieved a

Christian coalition in the nation. Although there had been many churches, unity of any kind had always been an elusive desire. Now, however, Christian unity was developing. This was not a pastoral unity based on fellowship and mutual care and discussions of doctrine. It was an apostolic unity addressing such things as politics, power, and the destiny of a nation.

The need at the moment was for money to place Christian candidates on the electoral ballots. I asked how much. My friend told me that it would cost $50,000 for each provincial governorship and $1 million for the presidency. I told him that I agreed it would be a good investment of $2.5 million or so which could turn out to be a small price for "buying a country"!

## Elections Cost Money

I hasten to say that this ambitious plan did not materialize, but I mention it here for a couple of reasons. First, it needs to be clarified that the proposal was not to buy votes, but the fact of the matter is that winning democratic elections fair and square does cost money. Even in a nation as accustomed to democracy as the U.S., no candidate need think of running for the presidency who cannot access $300-500 million in campaign funds. The second reason I bring it up is to highlight the fact that "buying a nation" is not traditional nuclear church language. However, the more serious we get about social transformation, the more serious we need to get about the realistic price tags.

Some are catching on. I was fascinated to read the report of an ICA (International Coalition of Apostles) Regional

Summit in Baltimore, Maryland led by John Kelly in 2006. One of the apostles present said, "If you want to take a city, you need to buy it! Own businesses, property, and whatever other opportunities you can find to build wealth." As we pray for our cities, it might be well that we begin to beseech God to open the doors for His people to move strongly into this kind of ownership.

## The Great Transfer of Wealth

Numbers of respected prophets have been hearing God concerning wealth. They are using scriptures such as Isaiah 60:11, *"Your gates shall be open continually; they shall not be shut day or night, that men may bring to you the wealth of the Gentiles"* or *"The wealth of the sinner is stored up for the righteous"* (Prov. 13:22). Since somewhere around the early 1990s, diverse prophets from different parts of the nation and of the world have been receiving God's word that a huge transfer of wealth is about to begin. Some of us will be ready to receive it and some of us won't.

## Unmasking the Spirit of Poverty

One of the most effective devices that satan has been using to keep the church from being ready to receive a great transfer of wealth has been the pernicious influence of the spirit of poverty. The church in general has been seriously deluded with the widespread notion that piety is closely related to poverty.

What does the Bible say? Deuteronomy 28 is one of the most enlightening chapters in the Bible on prosperity and poverty. Verses 1–14 tell of prosperity while verses 15–68 tell of poverty. Prosperity, for example, includes "plenty of goods," namely a large healthy family, increase in livestock, and bountiful agricultural production (see Deut. 28:11). These and many more benefits are termed "blessings." *"The blessing of the Lord brings wealth"* (Prov. 10:22 NIV). Poverty, on the other hand, is described as hunger, thirst, nakedness, in need of all things (see Deut. 28:48). These and many other disasters are termed "curses."

Putting this in the context of dominion theology, it is clear that God's desire for the human race is prosperity. Satan's desire is for poverty to prevail. He knows that *"the poor man's wisdom is despised, and his words are not heard"* (Eccl. 9:16). In heaven there is no poverty, only prosperity. Aiming for "Your will to be done on earth as it is in heaven," implies that we do all we can to see that people prosper. The spirit of poverty is a demonic agent of satan intent on preventing people from enjoying God-given prosperity.

One of the most effective tactics of the evil spirit of poverty has been to persuade Christian leaders that poverty is somehow noble. This mindset entered the church when Greek philosophy gradually replaced the biblical Hebrew worldview among church leaders around the time when Constantine was the Roman Emperor. As I mentioned in Chapter 2, the Greeks espoused "dualism," which postulated that there was a spiritual world and a material world and that the spiritual world was far superior. Issues of wealth were associated with the material world, and truly spiritual people were to avoid that as much as possible. That is why, when the monastic movement began around then, the monks were required to display their spirituality with vows of poverty, chastity, and obedience. While chastity and obedience are not as prevalent today, poverty unfortunately persists as a spiritual ideal.

## Prosperity in the Global South

This is true particularly in our Western churches, namely in Europe and North America and Australia. These are the older, traditional, mostly stagnant churches that Philip Jenkins calls "the North."[2] He contrasts them with the dynamic, cutting-edge, booming churches of "the global South." I have already described some of the differences that Jenkins finds between the two regarding satan and demons and miracles and spiritual warfare. There are also notable differences in the ways they view poverty and prosperity. Apparently the spirit of poverty is being overcome in the global South while remaining entrenched in many of our churches in the North. For one thing, church leadership in the global South is culturally much more aligned with the Hebrew way of looking at life than with Greek dualism.

Jenkins finds that "Around the world, many highly successful churches teach some variant of the gospel of prosperity, the controversial belief that Christians have the right and duty to seek prosperity in this world, to obtain health and wealth here and now."[3] He is accurate in calling the gospel of prosperity a "controversial belief." At least it is controversial here in the North. *Time* magazine, for example, ran a cover story under the title "Does God Want You to Be Rich? Yes, say some megachurches. Others call it heresy. The debate over the new gospel of wealth."[4]

This debate is directly related to the thesis of this book, namely the dominion mandate. One of my pillars supporting "Social Transformation" has to do with obtaining control of large quantities of wealth. Here in the North, leaders of the charismatically inclined evangelical churches relating to the Second Apostolic Age are closer in their way of thinking to the successful churches of the global South than they are to the traditional denominational churches of the North. The *Time* writers skillfully painted this picture by contrasting the views of two of the most popular preachers of the day, best-selling authors Joel Osteen and Rick Warren.

## Osteen vs. Warren

Joel Osteen, representing what could be seen as the apostolically friendly churches, is quoted as saying, "I preach that anybody can improve their lives. I think God wants us to be prosperous. I think He wants us to be happy."[5] To the contrary, Rick Warren, a Southern Baptist evangelical, says, "The idea that God wants us to be wealthy? There is a word for that: baloney. It's creating a false idol. You don't measure your self-worth by your net worth."[6] Time goes on to comment that the brickbats aimed at the gospel of prosperity usually come from evangelicals like Warren, nevertheless "the [evangelical] movement, which has never had a robust theology of money, finds an aggressive philosophy advancing within its ranks that many of its leaders regard as simplistic, possibly heretical, and certainly embarrassing."[7]

Back to the global South, Philip Jenkins raises the telling possibility that the anti-prosperity camp might find itself out of step with the rapidly multiplying churches of the poorer parts of the world. He quotes Kefa Sempangi, who reflects the Hebrew as over against the Greek mindset when he says, "A religion is true if it *works*, if it meets *all* the needs of the people. A religion that speaks only to man's soul and not to his body is not true. Africans make no distinction between the spiritual and the physical...If the gospel you are preaching does not speak to human needs, it is useless."[8]

Here is the underlying irony according to Jenkins: "For a Northern world that enjoys health and wealth scarcely imagined by any previous society, it is perilously easy to despise believers who associate divine favor with full stomachs or access to the most meager forms of schooling or health care; who seek miracles in order to flourish, or even survive. The Prosperity Gospel is an inevitable by-product of a church containing so many of the very poorest."[9]

## New Black Churches

African Americans, across the board, comprise one of the poorest demographic segments in our nation. However, Harry Jackson, author (with George Barna) of *High Impact African-American Churches*, reports that a disproportionate number of black Christians are currently being attracted to huge megachurches in virtually every metropolitan area of the country. These churches have overcome the spirit of poverty. They are entrepreneurial. What Jackson calls "the new black pastors" have no built-in aversion to prosperity. They believe in social transformation. "They're trying to restore the city through community outreach that includes housing, businesses, and multiple streams of income into the church. Yet they're equally committed to improving the moral values of their community."[10]

True to form, some of the traditional African-American Christian leaders criticize such new black churches as Jackson's Hope Christian Church in Maryland for preaching a prosperity gospel. Jackson responds: "For those civil right warhorses, such as Jesse Jackson and Al Sharpton, to say churches like ours have abandoned Jesus' call for social justice to preach a gospel of wealth shows how out of touch they are with the current needs of the black community."[11]

## Mammon Is the Adversary

If what we have been seeing in this book is correct, the one most threatened by Christians shifting their paradigm from poverty to prosperity is satan himself. Let's recall that each step forward toward retaking dominion of God's creation involves an equal step backward for the enemy. Since control of wealth will be such a determining factor in social transformation, satan has assigned one of his highest-ranking demonic powers to thwart it, namely Mammon. Jesus said, *"You cannot serve God and mammon"* (Luke 16:13). Many think that Mammon is a synonym for money. It is not. John Kelly and Paul Costa say, "Mammon is not just the love of money that people worship. When people worship mammon, they are actually worshipping a demon. It is the demon that causes people to love money."[12]

Some believers unfortunately do love money. But no direct correlation can be shown between prosperity and the love of money. Mammon can and does influence poor people as well as rich people. Yielding to Mammon will quickly disqualify a person from playing a key role in being entrusted with wealth for the kingdom. Mammon uses four subordinate demonic spirits in his attempt to entrap believers: (1) the spirit of greed; (2) the spirit of covetousness; (3) the spirit of parsimony (stinginess); and (4) the spirit of self-reliance. Every one of us needs to be on constant guard because these spirits are very subtle.

But Mammon does not have to be successful. The Holy Spirit is more powerful. *"He who is in you is greater than he who is in the world"* (1 John 4:4). Most prosperous believers I currently know are not serving Mammon. Some of them, however, have been entrusted with considerable wealth. This helps position them for the kingdom. Every prominent philanthropist of whom I am aware is rich. Their personal and their family's needs are cared for. They are positioned to serve others in a way that they could not if they were poor. One reason why Rick Warren can influence a whole nation like Rwanda is that his books have sold tens of millions of copies and have thereby produced wealth that he can use to launch and implement his vision. I once heard Apostle Pat Francis of Kingdom Covenant Ministries in Toronto say that her goal is to help every member of her church become a millionaire. She says, "Their mission is to obtain wealth with wisdom and prosperity for Kingdom purpose."[13] When they do, without yielding to the seductions of Mammon, think of the influence they will have for transformation. I personally know both Warren and Francis, and I have seen no indication that either has fallen into the trap of being influenced by Mammon.

## The Chain of Wealth Transfer

According to the prophets, great wealth transfer is soon coming for the extension of the kingdom of God, and I believe that we are to help prepare the way. A good first step, as we have just seen, is to bind and neutralize the power of the spirit of poverty. We must recognize that God's will is prosperity and that poverty is a curse. A second step is to build an infrastructure for receiving, caring for, and distributing the wealth to be released. It was several years ago that I believe God began showing me the big picture through what I like to call the four links of the chain of wealth transfer:

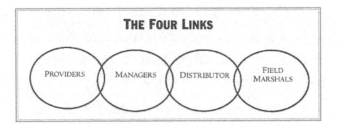

Each one of the four links in this chain—providers, managers, distributors, and field marshals—is significant. I personally would not anticipate the fulfillment of the prophecies concerning the transfer of wealth until all four of them are activated. This helps explain to some of us why the release of wealth, at least in the measure we have been anticipating, has not yet occurred. But the good news is that we have been making excellent progress in getting the necessary system into place.

## Field Marshals

Obviously, the objective is to get the wealth from the providers into the hands of the field marshals. The field marshals are those who are out on the front lines making things happen for the extension of the kingdom of God. They are healing the sick, casting out demons, saving souls, multiplying churches, caring for the poor and needy, and transforming society. Our two hundred years of modern missionary work, originating in the first world and developing later in the third world, have now put large numbers of field marshals in place.

While not all field marshals are equally effective in what they do, there are ways and means to identify the ones who are among the best. They have proven track records of skill, production, character, and integrity. I think, for example, of one in Africa who has been planting ten churches a day in several nations. I think of another in India who oversees no fewer than 15,000 church planters. Most of these field marshals could double or triple their successful efforts in extending the kingdom of God if they had more money. The purpose of the transfer of wealth is to attempt to provide them the material resources they need for optimum performance.

## Providers

The first link of the chain represents the providers. This is the initial source of the wealth that will be made available. It is important to recognize that providers do not necessarily need to be believers. Some will be believers, of course, but others will be providing the wealth of the unrighteous that has been stored up for the righteous as we saw above in Proverbs 13:32.

There are two general ways that this kingdom wealth will be released through the providers. Some of it will come through supernatural transfer of wealth that already exists. Some will come through the providers themselves receiving extraordinary power to generate new wealth. Let's look at both of them.

A well-known biblical example of the supernatural transfer of wealth is the Israelites leaving Egypt after being in slavery for four hundred years. While they were in the desert they were rich. Their wealth did not come from making bricks without straw. When they arrived in the desert they were unemployed. Their wealth came from their oppressors, the Egyptians, who were ungodly idol worshipers. It was not related to any production or financial skills that they might have had. True, the Israelites had to take action to receive what God was giving them. They had to send the women out to collect the valuables from their Egyptian neighbors. But the women didn't have to fight or argue or persuade their neighbors to give them the wealth. The power of God had moved on the Egyptians to such an extent that they voluntarily gave up the riches that they had accumulated. Pharaoh later regretted what they had done, but it was too late. God even supernaturally preserved the wealth of His people by drowning the pursuing Egyptians in the Red Sea.

To bring this up to date, Randall Sprague describes these kinds of providers as having the "Cyrus anointing." He says, "There is a group of people in the world today who by God's grace will penetrate the world's banking, finance, oil companies, 'old family' monies, organized crime, and drug money. They will come away with that wealth to evangelize the world, and they will be warriors."[14] The providers will be those who have had experience in handling large sums of money. They will not be novices. They will ordinarily be those whose personal and family financial requirements are secure. They will have little need to seek additional personal gain. They will have passed the basic tests of personal integrity and freedom from greed.

## Power to Get Wealth

The second kind of providers will exercise divine power to get new wealth. The Bible says, *"You shall remember the Lord your God, for it is He who gives you power to get wealth, that He may establish His covenant"* (Deut. 8:18). Unlike the supernatural transfer of wealth, the power to get wealth ordinarily relates to skills that the providers have developed. If they are in real estate, they will sell more than they have dreamed of. If they are making a 40 percent profit from their business they will make 100 percent next year. If they are engineers they will get new ideas for witty inventions. Those who receive this power will need to fulfill the two requirements of Deuteronomy 8:18: (1) They must remember the Lord and attribute their wealth to His provision, and (2) they must use the proceeds for establishing His covenant, namely for taking dominion.

## Distributors

The traditional system for financing the advance of the kingdom of God has been for the providers to supply the funding for the distributors. The distributors, the third link in the chain, are those who have established direct contact with the field marshals. In the old wineskin, distributors were typically denominational executives or mission board directors or leaders of specialized ministries. In the new wineskin, distributors are, for the most part, apostles.

Some providers, who have a vision for a certain ministry and who desire to be more hands-on, will start their own foundations and thereby assume the role of distributors as well as providers. Rick Warren would be an example. Perhaps the majority of providers, however, will shun the responsibilities of distribution. They prefer directing their energies and their creativity to increasing the flow of wealth. They trust experienced distributors, whom they have thoroughly checked out and whose vision they embrace, to disperse their funds wisely.

Traditionally, the role of distributors has been to hear from God, to cast the vision for their ministry, and to develop contacts with providers who will finance it. When there is financial need, they appeal to their donors for support, and the donors respond. The expectation is that the distributors will spend the money as they have promised whether it be for overhead or for new projects. Then when the money is gone, they make another appeal. This is called "donor-based financing," and it has been the norm up until now.

## Managers

I say "up until now," because I see an exciting new innovation on the horizon. This involves the second link in the chain, namely managers. The second link has been, by and large, the missing link. I would not be surprised to find that one of the reasons for the delay in the transfer of wealth that the prophets have been announcing is that the managers are not yet in place to the degree that God wants them to be.

For the most part, the managers will be workplace apostles who have experience in multiplying finances. Most of them will have developed skills working in the financial sector. I put them in the second link of the chain to indicate that, more and more, we will be seeing finances from the providers first going into the hands of managers before reaching the distributors. In this way much more wealth will be released. The divine "power to get wealth" of Deuteronomy 8:18 will be activated in anointed managers to extraordinary degrees. They will not be traditional financial planners who are satisfied with annual returns of 5 percent to 15 percent or so. I am dreaming of much more than that. I have faith that we will be seeing the biblical standard of 100 percent or more become a norm.

## The Parables of the Money Managers

"The biblical standard?" Many will be asking where I get the notion from the Bible that we could possibly expect to double kingdom money annually by legitimate means. My response is that it comes from Jesus' teaching. I refer to Jesus' two Parables of the Money Managers. The name doesn't immediately ring a bell because we are more accustomed to the traditional titles of these parables, namely the Parable of the Talents in Matthew 25 and the Parable of the Minas in Luke 19. These are two different stories with a great deal in common. "Talents" and "minas" were forms of currency in those days with a talent being worth about $1 million and a mina worth about $10,000. Both stories are set in the context of the financial market.

Jesus' point is that different people handle fund management in different ways, some good and some bad. In each story two of the three managers were commended for their trading skills. Check it out. Those who traded well in the story in Matthew 25 each gained 100 percent. Those in Luke gained 500 to 1,000 percent. True, we are not told what the period of time was, but in each case the boss simply went on a trip and came back. Chances are, their trips took something less than a year. Unless Jesus was purposely exaggerating for some reason that I cannot imagine, returns from the financial market of 100 percent and over per annum were not unthinkable to Him.

## Idle Money

The red flag for biblical money management is personified by the third manager in each of the stories. In one, he buried the money and in the other he wrapped it in a handkerchief and hid it. Neither squandered the money like the prodigal son; still they were considered *"wicked and lazy servants"* (Matt. 25:26). Why? Because they were satisfied with idle money,

money that should have been managed but was not. The principle is that kingdom finances should be multiplied as much as possible while they are being released. Unmanaged funds, stored at bank interest (scornfully referred to in Matt. 25:27) or even less for a future time when they might be needed will apparently not attract the blessing of God.

What was the problem with these disgraced fund managers? It was an irrational fear. In fact, it is well known that either of two opposite emotions can cripple fund managers—fear and greed. Greed was not an issue here as it is in other parables, but fear was. It was irrational fear because these individuals who failed in their duties were disloyal to their boss. They ignorantly accused him of reaping where he did not sow and collecting what he did not deposit. They used examples of farming and banking. But the boss was neither a farmer nor a banker. He was a trader. Where do the earnings come from in trading? They come from the market. It's very simple—those who trade well make money from those who trade poorly. This is nothing unethical; it is simply following the agreed upon rules of the profession.

## Revenue-Based Financing

The reason I have belabored this point is to highlight the crucial role of link number two, managers, in the chain of wealth transfer. What I envision is these workplace apostles taking the lead in facilitating a shift from what I described above as "donor-based financing" to a much more effective plan of "revenue-based financing." Ministries will establish revenue funds, the principal of which will not be spent for cash flow needs or new projects, but it will be skillfully managed. Contributions to the revenue funds will be regarded as investments in the ministry, not as donations to the ministry. As the revenue funds are managed, the investors will receive quarterly reports just as they would from Merrill-Lynch, even though it's the ministry's money, not their own. If they like what is happening to their money, they naturally will be inclined to invest more.

I have reason to believe that we will see ministry revenue funds matching Jesus' standard of at least 100 percent annual return. What this means is that a ministry with a budget of $1 million in overhead would set out to establish a revenue fund $1 million, the income from which would cover their overhead. In some cases, in order to anticipate inflation and possible expansion, they might choose to withdraw only 80 percent of the profits for operations and reinvest the other 20 percent. Instead of using donations for just paying the bills, they would then be free to use donations to launch new projects or to support other like-minded ministries. The key to making this happen, I repeat, is kingdom-minded financial managers to whom God will grant extraordinary power to get wealth.

Let's not only spend our money, let's multiply it before we spend it!

## Transformation of Jerusalem

One of the best-known biblical examples we have of a city being transformed is Jerusalem. During the seventy-year Babylonian captivity in which God was punishing Israel for idolatry, the once-magnificent city of Jerusalem became a deserted pile of rubble, a junk heap in modern terminology. However, it was eventually rebuilt. Jerusalem once again became a thriving city with commerce, a temple, walls around the city, and people living a good life. The process required about 100 years, but city transformation had actually taken place!

How did this happen? Two things were necessary: (1) individuals who were gifted by God and anointed for the task, and (2) wealth.

There were three prominent individuals whom God chose to lead His people: first Zerubbabel, then Ezra 81 years later, and finally Nehemiah 13 years after that. They were the ones entrusted with the wealth. Without godly people who have a vision for God's purposes, who have a heart to obey God, and who have proven integrity with finances, we cannot expect God to release large amounts of wealth.

The wealth for the transformation of Jerusalem was released through two pagan, idol-worshiping kings of Persia, Cyrus and Artaxerxes. This was a supernatural transfer of wealth, not the result of the Israelites' personal labor and production. It began when *the Lord stirred up the spirit of Cyrus king of Persia* (Ezra 1:1). Without the wealth of Persia, this classic case of social transformation could not have occurred.

As the days go by and as God's people continue to cast the vision for obeying God's dominion mandate, we can expect to see modern-day Cyruses and Artaxerxeses stirred up to provide astronomical amounts of wealth to be used for advancing the kingdom of God here on earth.

As Solomon says in Ecclesiastes 10:19, perhaps with his tongue in his cheek: "Money answers everything!"

# Chapter 10

# A NEW URGENCY: LET'S GET THE JOB DONE!

My desire in this brief concluding chapter is to help mold the pieces together into a whole. I am aware that the other chapters could, for the most part, be seen as free-standing essays on themes related to dominion theology. Each one, however, is intended to bring to our agendas a matter essential to a thorough understanding and practical implementation for our roles in helping to bring God's kingdom to earth as it is in heaven.

Each chapter is like a book in a dominion library. The bookends are the social transformation graphics that I showed in the introduction and that I will now display again:

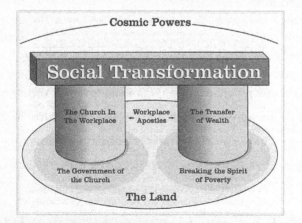

My approach will simply be to pick up the nine major themes of the book and show how they fit with each other to form the total dominion picture.

## 1. The Biblical Government of the Church

Three close friends of mine are currently working on other books dealing with social transformation or the dominion mandate. They, undoubtedly, are not the only ones. I am not aware of another time in history when such a thing was the case. Why is the time in which we live so different? I feel certain that it has to do with the Second Apostolic Age.

The biblical government of the church is the base for one of the two pillars supporting social transformation, but I also think it represents the tipping point time-wise. The awesome assignments that God is giving to the church in this season could not possibly have been undertaken without the activation of the foundation of the apostles and prophets. History will be different this side of 2001. The 21st century promises to be the most glorious century for the church this side of Jesus' death and resurrection.

## 2. Beyond Evangelism to Transformation

For over a century evangelical Christians stressed the evangelistic mandate while all but neglecting the cultural mandate. Saving souls and multiplying churches was our agreed upon goal. Yes, we fed the hungry and cared for orphans and provided hospitals along the way, but these were designed to open more doors for evangelism.

It is interesting to me that the graphic we are using has as the central bar Social Transformation and that evangelism and church planting do not even show up. This does not mean that they are excluded. More people are currently being won to Christ on a daily basis than ever before in history and the number will continue to go up. Missions and evangelism are now as much a part of the warp and woof of the church in general as taking communion or corporate worship or prayer, none of which needs to appear in a diagram representing current paradigm shifts.

We now understand that the kingdom of God is not confined to the four walls of the local church. We continue to be church people, but we are also kingdom people. The kingdom includes the church, but it is much broader than the church. We are now free to expect a literal answer to our prayer, "Your kingdom come, Your will be done on earth as it is in heaven."

## 3. The Desire to Take Dominion Is Biblical

It has taken a long time to outlive the stigma of "triumphalism" with which Constantine branded the church in the 4th century, but we now have open doors toward our understanding of what the Second Adam actually came to do. The first Adam lost the dominion over creation that God had given him and the Second Adam came to restore it.

Jesus came to "seek and to save that which was lost." What is it that was lost? Adam's dominion over creation.

We have now shed our inhibitions over theologizing about taking dominion. Dominion theology is not a flashback to

Constantinian triumphalism, but it certainly is a new call to action for a triumphant church. Dominion theology gives us a coherent understanding of what God has revealed in the Bible (*logos*) and what the Spirit is saying to the churches today (*rhema*). Taking dominion is not some kind of a grandiose human socio-political scheme; rather, it is the design of the Creator of the universe Himself for the future of the human race, which He put here on earth.

## 4. What We Choose to Do Really Matters to God

Of all the chapters, this one might come the closest in the minds of some to outright iconoclasm. To suggest that God honors our creativity enough to allow us to make certain decisions that He has not predetermined or even known ahead of time calls into question some of our most hallowed theological assumptions. It is hard to deny, however, that the Bible provides a great deal of revelatory evidence that God, indeed, has an open mind which He uses at His discretion. Most of us would agree that the Bible trumps theology. Seeing God as open minded is a legitimate, and I believe quite a convincing, way of understanding God from what He has revealed in His word.

If what we choose to do in obedience to God's commands has no effect on what God knows is going to happen anyway, I don't believe I would have a good enough reason to write a book like this.

If I may be allowed a personal speculation for a moment, it would be my opinion that open theism is the fifth most important theological breakthrough this side of the cross and resurrection. Is this an exaggeration? Possibly, but I don't think so. The other four would be: (1) The decision at the Council of Jerusalem that Gentiles do not have to be circumcised and become Jews in order to be saved; (2) Martin Luther's discovery of the biblical doctrine of justification by faith; (3) William Carey's insight that God expects us to use means to reach the heathen; and (4) the recognition of the true person and work of the Holy Spirit beginning with the Azusa Street revival.

## 5. The Spiritual Fuel for Taking Dominion Comes from the Holy Spirit

Speaking of the Azusa Street Revival of 1906, we can accurately say that the world has been different ever since. If dominion theology pulls together all the components of the social transformation graphic conceptually, the power of the Holy Spirit activates all of them operationally. It is no secret that the outworking of the classic doctrine of the Trinity has occupied professional theologians for centuries. Many of them still labor under a truncated pneumatology with no personal experience of the filling and the power of the Holy Spirit, but their number continues to diminish.

More and more we are recognizing the practical validity of what I said in Chapter 5—for the purpose of fulfilling the Great Commission, namely discipling the nations or transforming society, the immediate presence of the Third Person of the Trinity is more important than the immediate presence of the Second Person of the Trinity! Jesus is at the right hand of the Father making intercession for us. The operative power of God in our lives and ministries today is the Holy Spirit. That's why it is so unwise to quench the Spirit in any way.

## 6. Satan Is the Chief Enemy Who Must Be Defeated

Beginning in the Garden of Eden, the one being who stood in the way of Adam and Eve fulfilling God's destiny for them to take dominion of His creation was the serpent whom we know as satan. Satan will not let his usurped dominion of the kingdoms of this world go without a fight. We who believe in retaking dominion are engaged in this fight, commonly called spiritual warfare.

The decade of the 1990s was an accelerated learning experience for the body of Christ in matters relating to spiritual warfare, especially the strategic level of spiritual warfare relating to the principalities and powers that Paul refers to in Ephesians 6:12. Before then, concepts such as spiritual mapping or territorial spirits or identificational repentance were not even on our radar screens. But they are now, and they are extremely important for implementing social transformation.

Look at the graphic. Underlying the whole scheme is the land and related issues. Overshadowing the whole scheme are cosmic powers and related issues. Both of these are arenas directly related to spiritual warfare. Satan has polluted the land and cursed it. Satan has deployed high-ranking demonic powers to darken the spiritual atmosphere over society and to block the freedom of heaven flowing to earth. Both of these arenas need to be and can be cleansed spiritually. We have the tools to do it, we have the gifted personnel to do it, and we have the power of the Holy Spirit to do it. It will be done!

## 7. Our Work Is Our Ministry

Most of us used to believe that all ministry was done only in the context of the programs sponsored by local churches. No longer! We now know that God calls His people to minister in the workplace as well. One of the reasons why Kong Hee of Singapore pastors one of the largest churches in the world is that he teaches his people that they are not in the workplace just to make a living. He says that "We are to rule, dominate, take leadership, and exert influence in all the world. By wanting the whole earth to be filled with His glory, God expects maximum fruitfulness and productivity in everything that we do."[1]

The people of God are not only the church on Sundays; they are the church seven days a week. There is a form of the church in the workplace, and that church has a foundation of apostles and prophets. In the graphic, the only element with arrows signifying action are workplace apostles. If the Holy Spirit provides the spiritual fuel for social transformation, workplace apostles, those who can penetrate the seven mountains, are indispensable human agents for making it happen.

## 8. Let's Do Whatever Works

Through the years, some attempts to transform society have worked better than others. Let's learn from both our successes and our failures. We need to agree on a pragmatic approach to strategy if we expect to succeed. Our strategies of the past have been commendable, but few if any have led to sociologically verifiable transformation of a given city. Let's not condemn what we have done, but let's strive to do better.

One of the more promising strategic changes relates to the church in the workplace. It could well be that apostles of the workplace, if creatively activated, will turn out to be one of the strongest missionary forces that we have ever known. If they see their businesses as kingdom businesses they can move through doors that would never be opened to traditional missionaries, and their potential for catalyzing social transformation can be enormous. It is up to the body of Christ as a whole to recognize, affirm, support, and encourage apostolic workplace missionaries.

## 9. Transforming Society Costs Money

Make no mistake about it. If we do not have access to significant amounts of wealth, our attempts to take dominion will see minimal results. That is one reason why the apostolic workplace missionaries that I have just mentioned can play such a crucial role. God gives many of them the power to get wealth (see Deut. 8:18).

Furthermore, they have more experience in dealing with large sums of money than do most nuclear church leaders. They know how to manage. They understand the financial markets. They agree that idle money is a drag on extending the kingdom. They avoid the pitfalls of fear and greed. They have access to the seven mountains (religion, family, arts, education, government, media, business). With them in place, we can expect that God will release the wealth of the wicked that He has been promising—large sums of wealth that will be used to bring about significant, measurable social transformation.

## Conclusion

Those are the so-called "books" in the current dominion library. More undoubtedly will be added as we accumulate experience over the years. This is an exciting venture. It is exciting because it is rooted in the word of the Lord. It comes about as unfeigned obedience to what the Spirit is currently saying to the churches.

I know that many will join me as I close this book with an apostolic decree:

> *In the mighty name of Jesus*
> *And through the omnipotence of the Holy Spirit*
> *We decree on the authority of the word of the Lord*
> *that Your kingdom will come*
> *Your will shall be done on earth as it is in heaven!*
> *Amen.*

# NOTES

## Preface

1. Jon Mecham, "In God We Trust: Few in number, dominionists believe the Bible should govern society," Time, September 26, 2011, 38.
2. See http://www.tylwythteg.com/enemies/reconstruct3.html.
3. Kevin Phillips, *American Theocracy* (New York: Penguin Books, 2006), ix.
4. Rick Joyner, "The Kingdom of God Is the Strength of a Nation" (September 5, 2006), http://www.morningstarministries.org.
5. Quoted in Christianity Today editorial, "God's Will in the Public Square," September 2006, 28.

## Chapter 1 A New Wine: The Second Apostolic Age

1. Barrett actually lists six ecclesiastical megablocks, the sixth being "Marginal Christians" including Mormons, Jehovah's Witnesses, Spiritists, Occult, etc., a category that I am choosing to exclude.
2. David B. Barrett, et. al., "Missiometrics 2006," International Bulletin of Missionary Research, January 2006, 28.
3. The term "using means" might be unfamiliar to some. William Carey, a shoemaker in Britain, felt a strong call of God to go to India and reach the heathen to win them to Christ, to use terminology of that day. He presented his vision to a group of religious leaders, one of whom said words to the effect: "If God wants to reach the heathen, He will do it with or without your help. Please sit down, young man!" Carey persisted, wrote his renowned book, *An Enquiry into*

*the Obligation of Christians To Use Means for the Conversion of the Heathen* (1792), and went to India personifying the "means" that God would use to reach the lost.

## Chapter 2 A New Horizon: Social Transformation

1.  Bryant L. Myers, *Walking with the Poor: Principles and Practices of Transformational Development* (Maryknoll, NY: Orbis Books, 1999), 1.
2.  Joe Woodard, "Solving the secular paradox: How can Christians influence world culture?" Calgary Herald, Observer Section, B7.
3.  Personal correspondence with James D. Hunter, January 11, 2007.
4.  Brian Pickering, "Christian Influence on Australian Politics Clearly Growing," City Harvest Prayerlink, December 1, 2004, 3.
5.  H. Richard Neibuhr, *Christ and Culture* (New York, NY: Harper & Row Publishers, 1951), 171.
6.  Ibid., 171–172.
7.  Ibid., 217–218.
8.  Quoted in D. James Kennedy, "God's Purpose for Our Lives," Business Reform, July/August 2002, 17.
9.  John R. W. Stott, "The Great Commission" in , eds., One Race, One Gospel, One Task, vol. 1, (Minneapolis, MN: World Wide Publications, 1967), 50.
10. C. Peter Wagner, "Lausanne's Consultation on World Evangelization: A Personal Assessment," quoted in Waldron Scott, "The Significance of Pattaya," 74, in Jacob Thomas, From Lausanne to Manila: Evangelical Social Thought (Delhi, India: ISPCK, 2003), 117.

11. "Lausanne Occasional Papers No. 21 Grand Rapids Report: Evangelism and Social Responsibility: An Evangelical Commitment," (n.p., A Joint Publication of the Lausanne Committee for World Evangelization and the World Evangelical Fellowship, 1982), 25.

12. Luis Bush, "Transform World Indonesia 2005," privately published and circulated, 14.

13. Ed Silvoso, *Transformation* (Ventura, CA: Regal books, 2007), 115.

14. Ibid.

15. Sarah Pollak, "Guatemala: The Miracle of Almolonga," CWNews, June 10, 2005, CBN.com.

## Chapter 3 A New Paradigm: Dominion Theology

1. Notes taken from an address by Jim Hodges at "Starting the Year Off Right" conference in Denton, Texas, January 4, 2007.

2. Harold R. Eberle and Martin Trench, *Victorious Eschatology* (Yakima, WA: Worldcast Publishing, 2006), 1.

3. I would like to make it clear that premillennialism was used by God as a powerful motivating factor for missions in most of the 20th century. Allan Anderson, a foremost Pentecostal scholar, lists premillennialism as the first of five main features of global Pentecostalism. See "Spreading Fires: The Globalization of Pentecostalism in the Twentieth Century," International Bulletin of Missionary Research, January 2007, 8–14. However, we are now in a new season.

4. General Presbytery of the Assemblies of God, "Endtime Revival—Spirit-Led and Spirit-Controlled: A Response to Resolution 16," August, 2000.

5.  John Stott, The Lausanne Covenant: An Exposition and Commentary, Lausanne Occasional Papers, No. 3 (Wheaton IL: Lausanne Committee for World Evangelization, 1975), 36.

6.  Joseph Mattera, *Ruling in the Gates* (Lake Mary FL: Creation House Press, 2003), 5.

7.  Ibid., 49.

8.  Ed Silvoso, "Evangelism," Charisma, September 2004, 49.

9.  Myles Munroe, *Rediscovering the Kingdom* (Shippensburg, PA: Destiny Image, 2004), 26.

10. Steve Thompson, "Your Authority in Christ," The Morning Star Journal, Summer 2006, 22.

11. Joe Woodard, "Solving the secular paradox: How can Christians influence world culture?" Calgary Herald, June 19, 2005, B7.

12. Personal correspondence with James D. Hunter, January 11, 2007.

13. Donald Anderson McGavran, *The Bridges of God: A Study in the Strategy of Missions* (New York, NY: Friendship Press, 1981), 14.

## Chapter 4 A New Theological Breakthrough: God Has an Open Mind

1.  Doug Koop, "Closing the door on open theists?" Christianity Today, January 2003, 25.

2.  Ted Haggard, *Dog Training, Fly Fishing, & Sharing Christ in the 21st Century* (Nashville, TN: Thomas Nelson Publishers, 2002), 111.

3.  The Christianity Today issues were May 21, 2001 and June 11, 2001. The book is *Does God Have a Future?* by Christopher A. Hall and John Sanders (Grand Rapids, MI: Baker Academic, 2003).

4.  Christianity Today, May 11, 2001, 39.

5.  John Sanders, Christianity Today, May 21, 2001, 40.

6.  Ibid.

7.  Walter Wink, *Engaging the Powers* (Minneapolis, MN: Fortress Press, 1993), 298.

8.  Richard Foster, *Celebration of Discipline* (San Francisco, CA: HarperSan Francisco, 1988), 35.

9.  Brother Andrew, *And God Changed His Mind* (Grand Rapids, MI: Chosen Books, 1990), 15.

10. Jack Hayford, *Prayer Is Invading the Impossible* (New York, NY: Ballantine Books, 1977), 53.

11. Jack Hayford, "Pray with Power," Ministries Today, July/August 2003, 90.

12. Ibid.

13. Mary Alice Isleib, "Releasing God's Mighty Power," The Voice, July 2006, 12.

## Chapter 5 A New Vitality: The Power of the Holy Spirit

1.  See, for example, *Temporary Gifts: John Calvin's Doctrine of the Cessation of Miracles* by Beth Yvonne Langstaff (Ann Arbor, MI: UMI Dissertation Services, 1999).

2.  Robin McMillan, "The Kingdom Is Supernatural," The Morning Star Journal, January 2006, 9.

3.  Margaret M. Poloma, *The Assemblies of God at the Crossroads* (Knoxville, TN: The University of Tennessee Press, 1989), 94.

## Chapter 6 A New Reality: This Means War!

1.  Philip Jenkins, *The New Faces of Christianity* (New York, NY: Oxford University Press, 2006), 100.

2.  Ibid.

3.  Ibid., 98.

4. W. Gunther, "Nikao," *The New International Dictionary of New Testament Theology*, vol. 1, ed., Colin Brown (Grand Rapids, MI: Zondervan Publishing House, 1975), 650.

5. Ramsay MacMullen, *Christianizing the Roman Empire AD 100-400* (New Haven, CT, Yale University Press, 1984), 26. The quote is from Acts of John 38-45. Recognizing that some scholars question the accuracy of Acts of John, MacMullen argues that "Such wonderful stories were most reliably reported (Ibid., 26), and provides more historical justification in his footnote on page 133.

6. Dawn Europa, DAWN Friday Fax #43.01,9, November 2001.

7. See George Otis, Jr., *Informed Intercession* (Ventura, CA: Regal Books, 1999).

8. Dawn Europa, DAWN Friday Fax #43.01,9, November 2001.

9. Ibid.

10. Ibid.

11. Richard J. Foster, *Prayer: Finding the Heart's True Home* (San Francisco, CA: Harper SanFrancisco, 1992), 229.

## Chapter 7 A New Scenario: The Church in the Workplace

1. Lance Wallnau, "A Prophetic, Biblical, and Personal Call to the Marketplace" (n.p., privately printed, n.d.).

2. Laura Nash and Scotty McLennan, *Church on Sunday, Work on Monday* (San Francisco, CA: Jossey-Bass, 2001), 128.

3. Steven B. Sample, "President's Page," USC Trojan Family Magazine, Autumn 2006, 5.

4. "If I Had It to Do Over Again…A Rev! Interview with John Maxwell," Rev! Magazine, September/October, 2006, 36.

5. Ibid.

6. George Otis, Jr., Informed Intercession (Ventura, CA: Renew, 1999), 56.

## Chapter 8 A New Strategy: Learning from Experience

1. See *Ashamed of the Gospel* by John F. MacArthur (Wheaton, IL: Crossway Books, 1993).
2. Bryant L. Myers, *Walking with the Poor* (Maryknoll, NY: Orbis Books, 1999), 146.
3. Ibid.
4. Ibid., 146-147.
5. Ibid., 176.
6. Wesley Duewel, *Revival Fire* (Grand Rapids, MI: Zondervan Publishing House, 1995), 46.
7. Morris Ruddick, "Ruddick Update" response@strategic-initiatives.org, December 13, 2006, 2.
8. Michael M. Phillips, "In Swaziland, U.S. Preacher Sees His Dream Vanish," The Wall Street Journal, December 19, 2005, A1.
9. Ibid., A8.
10. Deann Alford, "The Truth Is Somewhere," Christianity Today, September 2006, 21.
11. Myers, Walking with the Poor, 128.
12. Carlotta Call (The New York Times), "Opium harvest increases 49%," The Gazette (Colorado Springs, CO), September 3, 2006.
13. Abram Book, "Giants in the Land," Leadership, Summer 2006, 18.
14. Ibid., 19.
15. Cited in *Marketplace Miracles* by Rick Heeren (manuscript, 158) to be published by Regal Books in 2007.
16. Ibid., 163.
17. Andrew Paquin, "Politically Driven Injustice," Christianity Today, February 2006, 88.
18. Charisma, "A Voice in the Wilderness," August 2006, 64.

19. Ken Eldred, *God Is at Work: Transforming People and Nations Through Business* (Ventura, CA: Regal Books, 2005), 46.
20. Ibid.
21. Ibid.
22. Ibid., 53.

## Chapter 9 A New Influence: Money Answers Everything!

1. John Kelly and Paul Costa, *Power to Get Wealth* (Hinesville, GA: Palm Tree Publications, 2006), 7.
2. See Philip Jenkins, *The New Christendom* (New York, NY: Oxford University Press, 2002).
3. Philip Jenkins, *The New Faces of Christianity* (New York, NY: Oxford University Press, 2006), 90.
4. Time, September 18, 2006.
5. Ibid., 53.
6. Ibid., 50.
7. Ibid.
8. Jenkins, *The New Faces*, 96-97.
9. Ibid., 97.
10. Edward Gilbreath, "High-Impact Leader and Shaker," Christianity Today, November 2006, 54.
11. Ibid.
12. Kelly and Costa, 41-42.
13. Pat Francis in personal correspondence, January 17, 2007.
14. Randall Sprague, *The Cyrus Anointing* (Tulsa, OK: Phos Publishing, Inc., 1998), 50.

## Chapter 10 A New Urgency: Let's Get the Job Done!

1. Kong Hee, "The Glory in You," Harvest Times, April-July 2006, 18.

# ABOUT C. PETER WAGNER

C. Peter Wagner was the Ambassadorial Apostle of Global Spheres, Inc. (GSI), an apostolic network providing activation and alignment for kingdom-minded leaders of the body of Christ. He traveled extensively throughout the world, helping to equip believers to minister in the areas of apostolic ministries, wealth, dominion, and reformation of society. Wagner considered this his "fourth career," which he began at the age of eighty. His first career was serving as a missionary to Bolivia, along with his wife, Doris; his second was teaching in the Fuller Seminary School of World Mission (now School of Intercultural Studies); and his third was founding and developing Global Harvest Ministries, which included the world prayer movement and the Wagner University. On October 21, 2016 Peter went home to be with the Lord.

# YOUR
# Prophetic
## COMMUNITY

## Are you passionate about hearing God's voice, walking with Jesus, and experiencing the power of the Holy Spirit?

Destiny Image is a community of believers with a passion for equipping and encouraging you to live the prophetic, supernatural life you were created for!

We offer a fresh helping of practical articles, dynamic podcasts, and powerful videos from respected, Spirit-empowered, Christian leaders to fuel the holy fire within you.

## Sign up now to get awesome content delivered to your inbox
### destinyimage.com/sign-up

 **Destiny Image**